MORE THAN 52 CHURCHES

THE JOURNEY CONTINUES

VISITING CHURCHES SERIES
BOOK 2

PETER DEHAAN

More Than 52 Churches: The Journey Continues

Copyright © 2020 by Peter DeHaan

Visiting Churches Series, Book 2

All rights reserved. No part of this book may be reproduced, disseminated, or transmitted in any form, by any means, or for any purpose without the express written consent of the author or his legal representatives. The only exception is short excerpts and the cover image for reviews or academic research. For permissions: PeterDeHaan.com/contact.

Unless otherwise noted, Scriptures taken from the Holy Bible, New International Version®, NIV®. Copyright © 1973, 1978, 1984, 2011 by Biblica, Inc.™ Used by permission of Zondervan. All rights reserved worldwide. www.zondervan.com The "NIV" and "New International Version" are trademarks registered in the United States Patent and Trademark Office by Biblica, Inc.™

Library of Congress Control Number: 2021914753

Published by Rock Rooster Books, Grand Rapids, Michigan

ISBNs:

- 978-1-948082-29-7 (e-book)
- 978-1-948082-30-3 (paperback)
- 978-1-948082-31-0 (hardcover)
- 979-8-88809-019-0 (audiobook)

Credits:

- Developmental editor: Cathy Rueter
- Copyeditor: Robyn Mulder
- Cover design: Taryn Nergaard
- Author photo: Chelsie Jensen Photography

To Kelli DeHaan

Books in the Visiting Churches Series:

52 Churches
More Than 52 Churches
Visiting Online Church
Shopping for Church
The 52 Churches Workbook
The More Than 52 Churches Workbook

For a list of all Peter's books, go to
    PeterDeHaan.com/books.

CONTENTS

Wasn't 52 Churches Enough? 1
Church #53: Home for Easter Sunday 4

MORE OPPORTUNITIES

Church #54: Emergent Maybe 9
Church #55: New and Small 15
Church #56: The Reboot 21
Church #57: Another New Church 27
Church #58: Not So Friendly 32
Church #59: Big, Yet Compelling 38
Church #60: A Missed Opportunity 47
Church #61: The Wrong Time to Visit 49
Church #62: Off to a Great Start 59
Church #63: We Don't Need No Sermon 64
Church #64: Is Bigger Always Better? 70
Church #65: Short of Meeting Expectations 78
Church #66: Gifts of the Spirit 87
Church #66, Part 2: A Normal Service 95
Church #67: Satellite Church 102
Church #68: Urban on a Mission 110

OTHER CONSIDERATIONS

Church #69: Suffering from a Bad Rap 121
Church #70: Unplanned and Spontaneous 123
Church #71: A Messianic Jewish Congregation 125
Church #72: Respected and Esteemed 128
Church #73: A Debatable Destination 130
Church #74: An Intriguing Mystery 132
Church #75: Fatigue and Fear Set In 134
Our Home Church 136

How to Be an Engaging Church	138
How to Go to Church	146
What Book Do You Want to Read Next?	152
For Small Groups, Sunday School, and Classes	153
About Peter DeHaan	155
Books by Peter DeHaan	156

WASN'T 52 CHURCHES ENOUGH?

For *52 Churches*, my wife and I spent one year visiting a different Christian church every Sunday. It was an amazing journey that allowed us to experience the vast scope of Jesus's church. The experience expanded our faith as we celebrated God in various local branches of his church. Yes, the worship practices varied and theology diverged, but the God behind these churches stood constant. It was good. So good.

We wrapped up the year in awe of God, appreciative of the diversity of his church, and grateful for the impact of the people we met along the way. We also felt relief (though mixed with a degree of sadness) as our journey concluded, and we celebrated a return to our home church on Easter.

In truth, visiting different churches week after week was exhausting. It wore us down. Even though our journey started as a fun adventure, toward the end it took more effort to walk into an unfamiliar church each Sunday with open eyes and fresh enthusiasm. Yes, we learned so much and met so many amazing people, both leaders and laity, but it was good to reclaim the regular routine of going to our home church every Sunday.

Still, I knew the journey wasn't over. We had more to do.

Yes, the fifty-two churches we visited were a diverse group. But by design, they were all within ten miles of our house. Expanding our journey will unveil greater diversity, new insights, and more to celebrate. Therefore, we'll look for more churches to visit, but we can't—we won't—do this every Sunday.

Instead, we'll plan our visits sporadically, as our schedule allows, while maintaining a firm connection with our home church. This time, however, instead of methodically selecting churches based on their distance from our house, we'll strategically choose them to realize the greatest range of experiences. This will maximize the scope of our journey and magnify our lessons.

But first, I'd like to share a couple of personal notes. As I mentioned in *52 Churches*, I'm an introvert—as is slightly more than half the population. Navigating new social settings challenges me. This includes visiting churches. Even though I never got past my apprehension of walking into a new church each Sunday, it did become easier as the year progressed, since visiting churches became our new Sunday norm.

This time, I expect visiting to not be as easy. Since these church visits will unfold at irregular intervals, my Sunday norm will be going to our home church. Visiting a church will be an anomaly. Therefore, despite having done so over fifty times, I anticipate walking into these churches to be more difficult, not less. I'll simply be out of practice and will encounter more—not less—emotionally laden moments.

Also, I want to affirm Candy, my wife and accomplice, for these visits. I couldn't have asked for more. Having her at my side for each of the first fifty-two churches made a huge difference. Throughout, she was a perfect partner on our journey. Each week she would contact the church we planned to visit, verifying key details. And each week she went without complaint, offering her full support to me and our adventure. This became our normal Sunday practice for a whole year, and her support was essential. This time, however, lacking a specific plan and schedule, we'll need to discuss where we're going and when. I anticipate some give-and-take that each marriage—each partnership of two people—encounters from time to time. Nonetheless, I know her support will shine just as brightly this time as last.

Having covered this, now I'm ready to start, but before we resume our church visitations, let's revisit our return to our home church, Church #53. We'll start with a condensed version of what I shared in *52 Churches*.

CHURCH #53: HOME FOR EASTER SUNDAY

Our journey of visiting fifty-two churches in a year is over. I'm sad and excited at the same time. Our reunion with our home church community looms large.

It's Easter, and we're returning to the people we love and have missed. I expect a joyful homecoming and a grand celebration: personally, corporately, and spiritually.

We arrive early to meet our kids. While our daughter and her husband attend this church, our son and his wife make an hour drive to spend Easter with us, beginning our day together at church.

I hope for a discreet return, but friends spot me right away. They're glad to see me but not sure if we're back for good. I confirm our adventure wasn't to find a new church. They're relieved.

Our reunion blocks the flow of people, so I excuse myself to find my family. Even arriving early, there aren't many places left for six, but they did find a spot. I sit down and soak in the ambiance.

There's nothing special about the building, except its age. Located in the heart of the downtown area, the sanctuary is over 150 years old, far from contemporary. Even with many enhancements, a dated feel pervades.

To start the service, our pastor welcomes everyone, telling visitors what the regulars already know: there's no plan for the service today, only a general intent. Its length is unknown, so it will end when it ends. He reiterates that we have freedom in worship: We may sit, or stand, or kneel. We may dance or move about—or not. As is our practice, children remain with their parents during the service, worshiping along with the adults, but often in their own way. There will also be an open adult baptism later in the service. With the place packed, he asks the congregation to slide toward the center of the seating to make room on the ends for those still needing seats.

The worship team starts the service with a prayer and then kicks off the first song. The energy level is high. After thirty minutes or more of singing we hear a brief message. The church is in a yearlong series—I've kept up by listening online and apprised Candy on key announcements and teachings. Today, the lesson is about Abraham and Sarah, her scheme for her husband to produce a child through her servant, and his boneheaded acceptance of her misguided plan. Our pastor ties this in with Easter: We all make mistakes, and we all need Jesus, who offers forgiveness and provides restoration.

Next is baptism. Our pastor shares the basics of the tradition. The rite is the New Testament replacement for Old Testament circumcision, which he addressed in the message. Baptism symbolizes the washing away of our sins, a ceremonial cleansing, which publicly identifies us with Jesus. Other creeds say baptism (by immersion) portrays the death, burial, and resurrection of Jesus. Can't it be both?

People desiring baptism may come forward as the worship team leads the congregation in more songs. Even before hearing the full invitation, one person walks forward and then another. A line forms.

For many churches, baptism is a somber affair, conducted with reserved formality. Not so for us. We treat it as a celebration with unabashed enthusiasm.

Our church leader prefers baptism by immersion, but the floor of this 150-year-old building lacks the structural integrity to support the weight of a baptismal pool. Instead, we use a traditional baptismal font, with the goal to get as much water on the recipient as possible.

After an elder douses the first person with water, a raucous celebration erupts from the crowd. We cheer this woman's public proclamation of faith. We baptize a dozen this morning, with more that will happen at the next service. What a glorious Easter.

With the baptisms complete, we resume singing. After a couple more songs, the worship leader concludes the service and the crowd slowly disperses. We eventually make our way out after ninety minutes. Some have already arrived for the next service, which starts in half an hour.

Today is an amazing reunion, a grand celebration, and a fitting conclusion to our yearlong pilgrimage.

Takeaway for Everyone: Is your church service a celebration or a stoic gathering?

MORE OPPORTUNITIES

With hundreds of churches nearby within acceptable driving distance, which ones will we select? We start by listing churches that we wanted to visit for the *52 Churches* project, but couldn't because they fell outside our 10-mile criteria. Now we can check them out. Next, we look for other churches that will give us greater variety: big churches and small, new churches and different faith expressions. We're willing to drive greater distances to explore greater variations in Jesus's church.

Armed with an initial list, we look for an opening in our schedule to resume our exploration of area churches. We don't need to wait long.

CHURCH #54: EMERGENT MAYBE

Someone once quipped, "There are more books *about* emergent churches than there are emergent churches." That seems like hyperbole, but my experience confirms it. I've read several books about emergent churches, but I've never actually been to one. Tonight's experience may change that, but I'm not sure.

My wife, Candy, and I have an opening in our normal Sunday evening plans. This is an opportunity to visit a site plant of our home church (Church #53, "Home for Easter Sunday"). They meet at 5:30 for a community meal and then have a service afterward—more or less.

For the past couple of weeks, we've discussed going. I'm in favor of it, but my bride is reluctant. It's not that she fears adventure, but she fears the neighborhood. I offer the suggestion, but I don't push it, hoping she'll agree to go, without me having to talk her into it.

Sunday morning, I'm still waiting. The decision happens as Candy talks with one of the site plant leaders. He's a friend and fellow writer. We hang out a couple times a month.

His plans for tonight are to share a meal, offer a brief teaching, and then go for a prayer walk in the neighborhood. I'm sure his intent to wander the streets surrounding the church building will discourage Candy from going. It's one thing to drive to a semi-safe area and scurry inside a building, but it's another to traipse around the neighborhood. (In all honesty, I'm apprehensive of the semi-safe prayer walk, too, but I'm willing to push through.) His words don't offer the assurance Candy seeks, but she asks what food to bring.

As visitors, they'd forgive us if we showed up empty-handed, but during our year of visiting fifty-two churches, we did our share of mooching, and I don't want to do so again. Vegetables, we learn, are typically lacking at their weekly potluck, so on our way home from the morning service, we stop by the store to pick up our contribution for the evening meal.

The building is familiar to us. It's the one our church first used until outgrowing the facility and moving. At first, a contingent of people remained, but our church leaders did poorly at managing multiple locations and eventually shut the site down. Now—wiser, better equipped, and armed with a new plan—a cadre has returned, intent on serving this underserved neighborhood: the area's poorest and least safe, crime-ridden and void of hope.

After a minor detour, because I made a wrong turn, we arrive right at 5:30. My all-too-familiar anxiety about confronting the unknown rumbles in my gut. My pulse quickens as we pull into the small, but mostly filled, parking lot. I want to make a U-turn and race home, but the likeli-

More Than 52 Churches

hood of my wife laughing at my panic steels my resolve enough to park our car. Another family exits their minivan, with kids in tow and food in hand. Feeling a bit assured, we follow them through the back door that leads directly to the lower level.

With only a handful of people present, there's even less food, mostly desserts. Round tables fill the basement. The one nearest us holds the food while one further away accommodates some people awaiting the meal. Between the two is a room of empty spaces, except for a solitary woman sitting at her own table. Pleasant-looking and approachable, my instincts are to talk to her, while mindful that she could misunderstand my efforts or feel uncomfortable. If I can get Candy's attention, we can go together, but she's at the food table, talking with someone who just emerged from the kitchen. To my relief, someone eventually joins the woman so she's no longer alone.

I scan the room, expecting to see friends who are part of this adventure, but I don't see them. From upstairs come sounds of the worship team practicing. Surely, some of my friends are there. Although I see a few familiar faces, I don't recall any names. While I survey the situation, one of the familiar faces comes up to talk. We have a friendly, yet awkward, exchange that lasts too long.

A small white dog meanders over to welcome me. I squat, offering my hand for him to smell. All he does is sniff and tremble. He doesn't withdraw, yet he's not advancing for me to pet him either. He's apprehensive and has found a kindred soul in me. I later learn his name is Beau, nicknamed Bobo. He serves as the church's unofficial mascot, esteemed by all, and cared for by many. He belongs to our friends: the site pastor and his wife. They welcomed Beau into their home and later adopted him. This is poetic preparation, for they will soon welcome a foster child into their home with the intent to adopt him too.

Eventually, the site pastor descends the stairs. Dismayed with the low turnout, he concedes we should not wait any longer for more to arrive. We gather in a circle and hold hands while he prays. He reminds us that sharing a meal is communion. As we eat and drink together, we do so to remember Jesus. With the *Amen* said, people surge toward the food table.

We've now grown in number to about thirty, yet the food hasn't kept pace, and it's still half desserts. Some people bought prepared food at the store, others share leftovers, and one person made some stew. It smells tasty but is gone before I get to it. I hold back, as do a few others. Some people may depend on this for their evening meal. If I don't have enough to eat, there's more awaiting me at home. Others may not have that luxury.

Candy and I sit at a nearby table with our food, and others join us. We get to know them, making connections as we eat. As a bonus, today is the birthday of one of our leaders. We sing to her and share cake.

My focus is more on the fellowship than the food. But I reckon they cut both short when they urge us upstairs. As we do, more friends show up. With four young children, it's too much work to get their brood's tiny mouths all fed before the worship time starts, so they eat at home and show up a bit later.

The sanctuary is different from the last time we were here some five years ago. The antiquated pews are gone, replaced with comfortable, padded chairs. The ambiance of the coffee house next to the sanctuary is gone with its accessories stripped away to provide only the most basic options. In the back, areas are set up for kids to play, with plenty of open floor space for physical worship. The overhead lights remain off, with mood lighting taking their place. The result is a peaceful, subdued setting.

There's a short teaching, though our leader misses his goal of keeping it under ten minutes. He references Exodus 14:19–22, speaking about slavery, drawing present-day parallels for us to contemplate. He wraps up about fifteen minutes later. With the planned prayer walk canceled due to a light rain, a time of worship starts, now an hour into the evening.

A few of the people from the meal are missing, but several more have arrived, swelling our group to over forty. Candy and I are at the upper end of the age spectrum. Most are in their mid-twenties and thirties, with a good number of children present.

The other site leader—the birthday girl—sits at the keyboard and leads us in song. A skillful and spirit-filled leader, she moves us forward with music. For some people the songs are the focus, while for others the sounds become reverent background music. Candy soon wearies of the repetition, repetition, repetition of the choruses. For me it's not the words that matter but the atmosphere: a worship space where we encounter God in multiple ways, according to each person's preference. Some people stand as they feel led, raising their arms, swaying, and reverently dancing. Others sit, bow, or kneel.

Some kids wave worship flags, praising God through solemn movement. A few adults join them. Other kids play quiet games, build with foam blocks, or create art on a wall-sized chalkboard. A couple of women dance in the back with graceful movement. I want to watch, worshiping God through the beauty of their motions, but I fear that in doing so I may intrude on a private moment between them and the Almighty.

The teaching pastor stands again, signaling his wife to pause her playing. He offers a bit of encouragement and instruction. We sing a final song, and he dismisses us with a traditional benediction.

The planned service is over, but no one leaves. Everyone tarries. We chat with several friends, offering prayers and blessings as needed. We say our goodbyes to the new friends we've made, thanking them for the opportunity to get to know them and wishing them well.

Many people attempt to leave, but they're unsuccessful. There are simply too many conversations to have. Among the first to exit, we leave at 8:00 p.m., two and a half hours after we arrived. The time passed quickly for me, as it does when I'm in the company of winsome Jesus followers. I relish the experience, suspecting this group is approaching a truer meaning of church than I've ever experienced on a Sunday morning.

Candy has a different assessment, saying that had she not already gone to church today, this would have left her wanting. This must be one reason why there are so many types of churches.

Regardless of our differing perspectives, I think we just had our first emergent church experience.

Takeaway for Leaders: Does your church do things differently to better meet the needs of the people you're trying to reach? If not, what must change?

CHURCH #55: NEW AND SMALL

One of our goals in *52 Churches* was to visit all ten churches located in our local school district. After *52 Churches* ended, that number increased to eleven. The primary marketing for this new church is yard signs, spread throughout the area, suggesting a different kind of church. We make a mental note to visit.

With another last-minute opening in our schedule, we have an opportunity to go there, but we can't remember their name—and the yard signs are gone. After some extensive online searching—investing much more time than any typical visitor would do—I stumble upon their name and find their Facebook page, but I can't locate a website.

Their Facebook page contains recent updates, but they don't mention service times or a schedule beyond their first two meetings several months ago. Now armed with their name, cyber sleuth Candy finds their website, which confirms their schedule and service time. They call themselves nondenominational, but their website describes a church that fits snugly within the evangelical stream of Christianity.

As an aside, I suspect most nondenominational churches are evangelical in function, since I've never been to one that wasn't. It's possible, however, for a church to include all three streams of Christianity. The service at Church #19 ("A Near Miss") seemed to embrace equal parts of traditional, evangelical, and charismatic churches. Even though they were part of a denomination (albeit a very loose one), their service felt the most nondenominational of any I've ever attended. They exemplified what I think nondenominational should be: open to anyone and everyone, without leaning toward a denomination or stream of Christianity.

We head out early. A winter storm blankets everything with a layer of ice. Several churches cancelled services, but we don't think to check if this one has. I pick a route that will be more traveled and hopefully less treacherous. Even these roads are slippery, and we shouldn't be out. Passing an accident confirms the folly of our adventure. The drive takes twice as long as normal.

The church is in a small strip mall. With only a couple of cars in the parking lot, I wonder if they, too, cancelled services. Supporting my suspicion, I don't see any lights or movement inside. The parking lot is even more icy than the roads. As we exit our car, a man calls out to be careful. With much concern, we inch our way toward him.

He introduces himself and doesn't bother to ask if we're visitors. He knows. With the weather, he expects low attendance and says they only have half of their worship team. Inwardly, I sigh. It seems that too often we show up when churches don't have one of their typical services.

Encouraged by the engaging welcome, we head inside. A

guy in the sound booth looks up and comes over to talk. He looks familiar and says the same to me. My bride notices he's wearing a clip-on mic and asks if he's the pastor. I wonder the same. He says, "Yes."

We've been at a church service in this space before. A couple of years prior to *52 Churches*, we visited Church #15 ("An Outlier Congregation") here. They since moved and changed pastors, which resulted in a much different experience for our *52 Churches* visit.

Today the room feels bigger than that visit several years ago. I suspect the prior church had one space in the mall, with the present configuration using two. They have 144 padded chairs, aligned in long rows. With only twelve people present, the vastness of the space makes our numbers feel even less. We're the oldest people there, with kids, teens, and younger adults all represented.

Even though we walked in two minutes late, we have time to talk with several people before the service. They finally start about fifteen minutes later. I'm not sure if beginning late is their norm or if they're allowing more time for people to arrive. As it turns out, it doesn't matter. We are the last to show up.

Today's worship leader normally plays drums, but today he fills in as worship leader for his older brother, who is working. He also plays guitar. Another guitarist and bassist join him. The drum kit sits idle. His leading is confident, though not polished. I've been to services where the worship team is so rehearsed that I feel I'm at a concert and miss worshiping God. The opposite is well-intentioned people who shouldn't be leading music. Their efforts unfold as a painful ordeal, repelling me from God. Today, we hit that ideal place between the two extremes. At least it's ideal for me. We sing several current worship songs, which draw me to God.

Then they have a time of sharing.

When churches do this, I often wonder why. One of three patterns usually emerges:

They call attention to the person sharing, as in "I just bought a new Lexis. Pray that my BMW sells so I can give money to the mission."

Or it borders on gossip, as in "My brother-in-law didn't come home again last night. My sister might file for divorce and seek full custody of the kids."

Third is a wish list to God, as in "Pray for a new job, a good-paying job, one where the boss treats employees with respect, and a new car to get me to work, suitable work clothes, and money for . . . "

Yeah, I'm exaggerating a bit, but not too much.

Not so at this church. They share well. My first hint of this is tissue boxes scattered throughout the room. Certainly, people shed tears here. My assumption proves correct. When the first two people share, both end up crying as they reveal the angst of their heart. Their words are not just a lament but also a testimony, teaching and encouraging others.

They remind me of Paul's words to Jesus's followers in Corinth, that each person should do their part in building up the church (1 Corinthians 14:26). Their time of sharing doesn't fully match Paul's instruction, but they come closer than I've ever seen before.

After several people share, the pastor asks for others to do the same. His words go beyond being polite. He's almost imploring more people to participate. I wonder if he's leaving an opening for Candy or me to say something. At his second request, I squirm a bit, but he doesn't prolong his plea. With no more takers, he moves on to his message.

It's the Sunday before Christmas, and he reads about Jesus's birth from Luke 2:8–14. The pastor has a gentle delivery, kind and accessible. Though it's not his fault, I have trouble concentrating on his words. I jot down a few verses and one sentence that strikes me: "God sent Jesus here so we could better understand his nature." I ponder this, missing what comes next in the sermon. I don't think of helping us understand his nature as one of Jesus's goals, but I realize the pastor is correct. How could I have missed this?

The service ends with more music, and then everyone hangs around to talk. Eventually, we interact with every adult present and several of the braver teens. We learn their leader is a tentmaker pastor, following Paul's example of working his trade to provide for ministry (Acts 18:2–3).

This, I feel, is how it should be, not expecting paid clergy to serve members but for members to minister to each other. If we rightly serve and minister to one another, as the Bible teaches, the role of pastors becomes much less demanding—almost unneeded. With less demand on their time, pastors won't need to work as much or receive compensation, with each paying their own way. We also learn many members have a charismatic background, but they're careful to avoid excess, doing all things properly, as Paul taught in 1 Corinthians 14:27–28.

As we talk, the lead guitarist has a bit of a jam session. "I really enjoy your playing," I tell him later, "but I suspect you were holding back!"

He smiles. "I didn't receive the set list until last night. Since I live in an apartment, I couldn't practice."

Having talked to everyone, we finally head out, the first

to do so, glad for the experience. Most of the ice has melted, and the roads are now fine. Our church experience today was a good one. This church does so many things right. I wish more people were part of it.

Takeaway for Members: How well do you do at ministering to one another? Or do you expect your paid clergy to do that?

CHURCH #56: THE REBOOT

We planned to visit this congregation for *52 Churches* but couldn't—because they didn't exist then. Back then, two churches—one we skipped and one we visited (Church #25, "Embarking on a Metamorphosis")—planned to simultaneously shut down for a few months and then reopen as a new, merged entity. It took more than a few months, and they didn't start their services until after the original *52 Churches* project ended.

As they moved forward, the process went by various names, but for simplicity I'm calling it a reboot. Along the way, two other churches joined in, sending people and support. Today, we'll see the results, eight months after their launch.

The large parking lot has ample room, but it also looks full. It's a nice sight. A warm day, people mill about outside, including two greeters by the entrance, bantering with all who pass. One opens the door for us.

Inside is a bustle of activity, almost chaotic—at least to

the uninitiated. As our eyes transition from outdoor glare to indoor normal, we pause to take in everything. There's a nursery check-in station, a table for missions, and another for visitors, but we don't make it that far. A woman greets us. We connect with each other, but, as our conversation wanes, I wonder what to do next.

"Oh, nametags," she says. "Do you want a nametag?"

"That'd be great." But I'm not sure she hears me.

"We all wear nametags here." She gestures to her own and guides us to the nametag table. By the time we finish, she's disappeared, and a line has formed behind us. With no room in the lobby to mingle, we have two choices. We can turn right to the fellowship hall and socialize, or head into the sanctuary and sit. We didn't arrive as early as I wanted. The service should start in a couple of minutes, so we walk straight ahead and choose our seats.

The floorplan of the facility remains the same; however, the lobby received a makeover, and the sanctuary underwent a complete transformation. Gone are the pews, organ, and more formal elements. In their place are padded chairs for a couple hundred, a stage for the musicians, and a contemporary altar. What once approached stodgy is now chic. Subdued lighting adds to the allure. I'm quite sure something special awaits us.

A countdown clock, displayed on dual screens, implies the service will begin in two minutes and thirty-two seconds. While some churches employ this as an absolute trigger to launch the service, for others it's a mere guide. Based on how organized they are, I expect the first, and I'm correct. With twenty seconds remaining, the worship team starts playing softly. There are two on guitars, one who's also the lead vocalist, another patting the congas, and a fourth who sings backup vocals. Their sound is light contemporary. When the singing starts, a few people stand but most don't. Slowly, others rise to join them and by the end of the first verse, most are standing, including Candy and me.

Changing the order today, communion—something they do every Sunday—follows. The program—they're careful to not call it a bulletin—says communion is open to "anyone who acknowledges Jesus Christ as the risen Savior." Children are welcome to take part, too, as determined by their parents or caregivers.

In the pre-communion teaching, the minister, a thirty-something hipster, talks about mercy and grace. Mercy is not receiving the punishment we deserve, while grace is receiving the good that we don't deserve. I like these simple explanations and use them often, but I've never contemplated them during communion. As I do, I realize how perfectly they fit. Jesus exemplifies both mercy and grace. Communion celebrates this.

There are two communion stations, one up front and one in back, to serve the 160 or so present. The method is to dip the bread in the juice and eat, either at the communion station or later in our seats. As the worship team plays, we may go up whenever we want, but for most that means right away. Candy and I sit, conspicuous by our inaction, as the throng surges forward. I try to concentrate on what I'm about to do, but as the only people still sitting, most of my effort focuses on not fidgeting. I sense my bride is anxious too.

After most of the people finish, we get in line. When it's her turn, Candy breaks off some bread, while the man holding the cup says something appropriate.

Candy dips her bread and pauses. Normally, we celebrate communion as a couple, eating it together as I declare Jesus's gift to her while she agrees. When it's my turn, the man says something different to me. Perplexed, I mumble a disconnected response. I dip my bread and Candy waits for me to say something. Today no words come, and I eat the bread without her. She follows. She seems disappointed over my break from our practice. She should be. I know I am.

Once again, I fail to fully embrace the wonder of what Jesus did. I went through the motions of communion, but failed to commune with God or my wife. We were the last to take communion, and now I just want to sit as quickly as possible.

I shake off my failure at communion as a children's choir sings. There are twelve girls and one boy. Today is Mother's Day, though the song doesn't follow that theme, but I'm not really listening. I'm more taken in by the animated antics of their leader. Bubbling with expression, she leads them well—and entertains me. Afterward, they distribute carnations to all females, "honoring all women." This nicely avoids the risk of having a celebration of mothers that inadvertently disregards those who desperately long to be moms but aren't. Candy doesn't like carnations, but she accepts a red one.

Then all the children come forward for a blessing. The pastor says, "Let's talk to Jesus." I appreciate his simple, kid-appropriate reminder of what prayer is. Then the congregation sings "Jesus Loves Me" as the kids head off for their classes.

For the offering, the minister reminds us, "Giving is an act of worship." This again strikes me as profound, just as it did the first time I heard it at Church #13 ("A Dedicated Pastor Team"). Even so, every Sunday during my teens, I heard the phrase "Let us worship God with our tithes and offerings." It meant nothing to me then. I assumed it was merely a polite euphemism for "give us your money." I understood the offering as merely a way to fund the church, and I missed it as worship.

The church is in the middle of a series about the importance of rest. Today's message is "Abide, Grow, Fruit, Prune," based on John 15:1–8. The goal is to produce fruit: the fruit of the Spirit (see Galatians 5:22–23), good deeds, and transformation. The minister asks, "Are you bearing fruit?" As the text reminds us, apart from God we can do nothing (John 15:5). Abiding will produce fruit. Rest will result in good works. We need to "find a place of rest," says the pastor. We will have "cycles of pruning and of growing." He ends with the advice "to rest in Christ."

The worship team plays softly as we exit the sanctuary. One man introduces us to some of his friends. He's outgoing, with an engaging personality. We talk at length. He says sometimes he's a greeter. Other times his role is to mingle and interact with visitors. Today he has the day off.

"You're doing it anyway!"

He smiles. "Yes, I guess I am."

"When you're serving where you should be, it comes naturally and gives life."

He nods, and Candy adds, "But trying to serve in the wrong place is never good." We acknowledge her wisdom.

Eventually our conversation wraps up. As I turn to leave, I spot the worship team at the communion table serving themselves communion. It's beautiful.

Despite the changes made in the facility's appearance, the service unfolded like most others. They merely housed typical expectations in a new package, updating the form but not the format.

We exit the sanctuary and, once again in the lobby, we have two choices. Head to our car or veer into the fellowship hall for food and more conversation. We stay and enjoy both.

For an eight-month-old church, they have much to offer: many who are involved, several programs and areas to serve, and great community. May God continue to bless them.

Takeaway for Everyone: When you're serving where you should be, it comes naturally and gives life.

CHURCH #57: ANOTHER NEW CHURCH

During our *52 Churches* journey, many people suggested we visit today's destination, but with their location falling outside our self-imposed ten-mile limit, we skipped them—all the while feeling we were missing something. When the building's former occupants became too few to carry on, one of the area's largest churches (Church #52, "Playing it Safe") took over the building with the intent of it becoming a second location. The people they sent there, however, eventually decided to start a new church. Today, we'll see the results.

The building is visible from the Interstate but not so accessible. It's hard to get to, with no direct route available, but we finally make it. Once we arrive, there's a circular drive around the building. Even though a sign, albeit too small to easily read, directs some traffic left and others right, my instinct is to drive counterclockwise. I think the main entrance is to the left, but I can't overcome my compulsion to go right. Fortunately, it works out.

As we walk to the building, I enjoy the warm sun and gentle breeze, a nice counterpoint to our cold, wet weather of the past few days. I spot friends, and we talk a bit before they head off to their small group meeting. Then we see another acquaintance and chat some more. Once we sit down, a friend of Candy's comes up and talks at length.

The sanctuary is nearly a cube. Its vaulted ceilings, supported by massive arched wooden beams, provide an impressive, open feel. Up front is a spacious stage, not grand but most functional. Behind us is a balcony. The main floor has about 250 padded chairs, with about one hundred people using them.

Five musicians begin to play: two guitars, a bass guitar, drums, and baby grand piano. This signals the service is about to start. Candy and her friend continue talking. I try to listen to their conversation, but I want to take in the music too. The band's driving sound draws me. Reminiscent of grunge, an unexpected harmonica provides even more intrigue. This church has a reputation for its many talented musicians, and I'm witnessing the results.

As the prelude winds down, we start the service in surprising fashion. One of the members gives us an assignment: break into groups and answer the question, "What is the purpose of church?"

I look at the stranger to my left, the only one close enough for a group. I extend my hand. "Hi, I'm Peter."

"I'm Lisa, and this is my son, Jordan."

"Hi Lisa. Hi Jordan." When Jordan ignores me, I turn back to Lisa.

"How long have you been coming here?" she asks.

"One week!" I flash a crooked grin, something I do well. "We're visiting."

She laughs and then becomes serious. "So, what is the purpose of church?"

"This is something I've given a lot of thought to." Despite extensive contemplation, I don't have a pithy one-liner to share. However, that doesn't stop me from trying. I think out loud. "The purpose of church is to form spiritual community." That's a good start, but there's much more: serving, outreach, giving, worshiping God, and mutual edification. The list goes on in my head.

Then my mind races to what church shouldn't be. It's not a place that entertains, serves me, meets my needs, or feeds me spiritually—that's *my* job. It's not a one-hour-a-week meeting or an obligation to fulfill. I want to say something snarky about sermons, too, but decorum prevails. This is good because I later learn her husband attends seminary.

Our discussion has just started when the leader tells everyone to wrap things up. I tune out the lengthy set of announcements that follow. I'm still thinking about what else I should have said. Church needs to have an outward focus, but we can't ignore an inward component either. What I am quite sure of is that true church seldom happens Sunday morning. I'm convinced it's a mere distraction to what God desires for us to experience.

Calm down, Peter. Don't get yourself worked up.

The musicians return to the stage, along with three backup vocalists. The lead vocalist plays piano. Curiously, she has her back to us. Her voice is strong, but I have trouble following since I can't see her face. Her seven compatriots face the congregation. Why doesn't she? If the intent is to remove them as the focus and let God receive our attention—a goal I heartily support—then why are they even on the stage? This so unsettles me that I struggle to sing, failing in my worship of God.

They're in week two of a series: "The Big 'C' Church." Today's installment is "The Purpose of Church." Their minister is gone, with the intern filling in. He's comfortable in front of a group, speaking more as a teacher than a preacher. He also attends seminary, and what he shares seems plucked from the classroom.

He imparts a string of Bible verses and theologically intriguing soundbites, but I fail to grasp their connection with each other or how they relate to the purpose of church. I learned more during our thirty-second group discussion than from him. The fault could lie with me. Or did he try to cram too much into his talk or do his presentation skills need work? Regardless, I leave still pondering the purpose of church.

The worship team plays softly to end the service, while the prayer team comes forward to pray for those who seek prayer. I talk more with Lisa. Her husband joins us. He attends the same seminary as today's speaker.

"What do you plan to do when you graduate?" I ask.

"I'm willing to go wherever God sends me and do whatever he asks." Then he grows somber. "So far, I don't know."

"What would you *like* to do?"

"Well, I don't want to preach. I'm leaning toward small groups or discipleship ministry. Or ministry that involves one-on-one interaction. I'm waiting for God's direction."

I nod. "Usually, he only tells us one step at a time."

He smiles in agreement.

Before he heads out, I bless him and his studies.

I find another friend. I sense I'm supposed to pray for

him. He wants prayer, but not in the area I assumed. He receives my prayers for his future and for wisdom. The second service is about to begin. Candy's waiting for me. When the music starts, we hustle out of the sanctuary.

We had rich interaction with people before and after the service. Yet they were people we knew. I wonder about our reception had we not known anyone. Our only other conversation was with Lisa and her husband, something that may not have happened if not for the assignment at the beginning of the service.

I think we need to return to better understand this church. I suspect they have much to offer, but I don't feel any compelling reason to come back and find out.

Takeaway for Members: Seek meaningful conversations before and after church, especially with visitors and people you don't know.

CHURCH #58: NOT SO FRIENDLY

Today, we head to one of the area's larger churches. In the past, they had a visible presence, but I've not heard much about them recently. Their website boasts that we'll find "a warm and friendly group of people." I bristle. It's like telling someone you're humble or you're honest: if you have to say it, you probably aren't. Experience tells me they'll try to be friendly but will fall short.

Their "First Impressions Team," sporting blue name badges, will be located "throughout the building" and available to answer questions. I suspect I should dress up, but their website says to "come as you are." What a relief.

I can't tell it from their website, but I know they're a charismatic church, part of the Assemblies of God denomination. Even their name obscures that fact. Their website has only one mention of their affiliation, which is in small type at the bottom of one page.

So many of the charismatic churches we've visited have

left me disappointed. I wonder what today will bring. I see a photo of their lead pastor. He's a thirty-something hipster and not at all what I expect for a church with reputed conservative leanings. With this enigma confronting my mind, my anticipation for their service heightens.

The church facility enjoys a visible presence with easy access from the Interstate. We follow the arrows for visitor parking, but we don't find it. So we park where everyone else does, glad for a spot under a shade tree, which will keep our car cool on this warm July day.

Always anxious before visiting a new church, today my gut churns even more, and then a sharp pain surprises me. My heart thumps. In near panic, I fight the impulse to flee. Unaware of my anxiety, Candy presses forward, and I fall in step alongside her. *It's going to be okay.* I begin to pray. By the time we reach the door, my breathing is back to normal, and my pulse has slowed. I'll be all right. Thank God!

Two greeters stand at the nearest entrance. The pair smiles broadly and holds open the doors. "Welcome youngsters!" The man is twenty years or so my elder. I wonder if this is his attempt at flattery or if we represent youth to this congregation. While we have been the youngest people present at too many churches, I don't expect that to happen today.

"I don't know you," says the woman. Affable, her directness carries an edge.

We admit to being first timers and exchange names. I don't catch theirs, and I doubt they remember ours. We soldier on in. Despite people milling about, all act preoccupied. Once again, we're invisible. We walk slowly, giving people time to approach us, but no one does. And we see no one for us to approach, either. Where are those blue-name-tagged "First Impressions" folks mentioned on their website? We have yet to see one.

Based on the facility and decor, I expect an usher handing out bulletins, but there isn't one. With nothing else to do, we stroll in and sit down.

The large sanctuary seats about eight hundred on the main level. The sloped floor and auditorium seating, although contemporary in intent, gives a stoic vibe. There's also a balcony, but, unlit, it must be closed. With only a smattering of people sitting down, they're not even close to needing it.

A countdown timer on dual screens tells us the service will begin in a few minutes. At some churches the counter signals the launch of the service, while at others it serves as a mere guideline, an anticlimactic tease. Today it is both.

The worship team of nine begins leading us in song when the display hits zero. Most of the people, however, aren't ready to worship. Many aren't even sitting down. Conversations continue as the band plays. Just as I'm settling into the chorus of an unfamiliar tune, a reunion between two people occurs to my left, with their loud conversation distracting me well into the third song. *I want to worship God. I must focus on the words I'm trying to sing.* Even so, focus evades me. I can't worship.

The band boasts three on guitar, with an electric bass, keyboard, and drums. Three vocalists round out the group. The vocals balance nicely with the instruments, though they've cranked the overall volume too high. Most disconcerting, however, is the subwoofer that sends out sound waves to press against my chest with each beat. It causes me discomfort, but Candy can't feel it.

Eventually we end up with about three hundred people,

half of whom wander in well after the service starts. They're mostly older than us, with few families and no children that I can see. By the end of the fourth song, the flow reduces to a trickle. Is worshiping God in song not important to them or was this just a prolonged prelude?

After ten minutes, with most everyone finally seated, the lead pastor welcomes us. He's everything I expected. I can't wait to hear his message. His open, casual demeanor is geared toward visitors, yet his occasional use of church jargon would leave the unchurched confused. I wonder how much of my speech is likewise salted, despite my efforts to purge my words of Christianese.

He refers to the bulletin, and I'm irked no one gave me one. I can't look at the section he mentions or read the additional information. Then he sits down as a series of video announcements play.

When he returns to the stage, he leads us in communion. "Everyone is invited to the table," he says, "to encounter Jesus in their own way." He explains the process, so we know what to expect. They serve both elements on one platter. The "bread" is small oyster crackers. As for the clear liquid, I wonder if it's white wine or clear grape juice. This is the most inclusive communion service I've ever experienced.

As a teetotaler, communion wine unsettles me, and I brace myself for its assault. It turns out to be grape juice, but my preoccupation over it fully distracts me from celebrating communion as I want.

We sing some more, and then the senior pastor introduces the guest speakers. I groan, hopefully to myself, at this news. I really wanted to hear their pastor, not some missionaries. But theirs isn't a typical missionary message. Instead, they share their story of how God prepared their future restoration even when they were in the middle of deep turmoil.

They are effective communicators. God's work in their lives is compelling. I jot down three one-liners: "Storms in life are inevitable," "God is present in the storms," and "May we see God's hand in the center of our storms." Though the message doesn't apply to me now, it one day might. I'm glad to know their story of hope.

Afterward, the senior pastor returns to the stage and introduces the offering. The ushers pass the offering plates with quick efficiency, yet they somehow miss a few rows. Miffed because they skipped him, one man chases down an usher so he can present his gift. Having completed his mission, the man returns to his seat while the pastor asks the prayer teams to come forward after the service to be available for prayer. As for himself and the rest of the staff, they will scoot out for their monthly visitor reception. The service ends, and most people scatter.

Candy thinks she sees someone she knows and goes over to investigate. I tarry, waiting to meet the man at the other end of my row, but he's already talking to someone else, and it seems it will be a long conversation. I scan the auditorium but see no one I can approach, and no one comes up to me. Soon I'm standing alone, with a gulf of emptiness around me. Not wanting to look too pathetic, I meander over to Candy. As I do, I look for the prayer teams up front but see no one.

After my wife wraps up her conversation, we head toward the door.

"We could check out the visitor thing," says my bride, "but why bother? We'll never be back."

I'm relieved. "Good point."

We didn't hear their lead pastor speak, but we did hear a worthy message, one that will stay with me. I'm glad to know this couple's story of God's provision and restoration. From that standpoint, the hour-and-forty-five-minute service was worth it, but the rest of our time here left me disappointed. I didn't worship God today or experience Christian community. I walk out feeling lonely.

At the door stand two people with blue nametags, the first ones I noticed all morning. At least now I know what the tags look like. Pleasant folks, we say our goodbyes and step out into the warm sunshine.

Takeaway for Everyone: Do you merely say you're a friendly church or prove it through your actions?

CHURCH #59: BIG, YET COMPELLING

One of the area's megachurches has intrigued me for years. At one time I was a regular podcast consumer of their weekly messages, which usually featured their founding pastor. A gifted communicator, he conveyed truth with a fresh voice and looked at spirituality from new vantage points. His perspectives moved me toward the spiritual *more* that I sought and helped satiate the angst in my soul. At the same time, he opened the door to more questions, good questions. Questions that pointed me to a more holistic pursuit of the God revealed in the Bible.

I longed to attend this church and experience him in person. Our first opportunity to visit came several years ago —long before the original 52 Churches project. We were out of town and planned our return trip to put us in the right place, at the right time for their second Sunday service. We got up early, grabbed a fast food breakfast, and hopped on the highway.

The balmy spring day, coupled with expectation for

More Than 52 Churches

what awaited, bolstered my anticipation as the miles ticked off. As we neared our destination, my exuberance, however, yielded to worry. The drive was taking too long. *We're going to be late!* Unexpected Sunday morning traffic didn't help.

After pushing the speed limit for the last forty-five minutes, we pulled into their parking lot five minutes early. I sighed, relieved it would all work out. But the packed parking lot didn't have a single open slot. Frustration mounted as I drove around, praying to find a spot as precious seconds ticked away. At last I saw someone head to their car, departing late from the first service. I drove to their spot, slipping into it as they left. Relief replaced frustration.

Still, we had a long walk to the building. We strode with purpose to the nearest entrance. The parking lot overwhelmed me, but inside the building my understanding of overwhelmed was redefined. The throng of people pulsated in all directions, providing a maze I could barely navigate. The church occupied an old mall, with our entrance far from our intended destination. I pushed onward—with my bride in tow—weaving my way between the press of people. Some flowed with me, but most had other intents.

Eventually the passageway opened, providing three options, with none more obvious than the others. The service should be starting now. My heart thumped. Which direction should we head? I spotted an information booth and knew my answer was nearby.

"Where's the sanctuary?" Panting and in a rush, I surely wasn't the friendliest of people.

The woman smiled and gave me a calm, reassuring look. "Is this your first time here?" She wanted to engage me in conversation, something I'd have welcomed if there had been more time.

I nodded, gasping for air. "Where's the sanctuary?" I knew I was being rude and that the young lady had valuable information to share, but right then I had a different goal.

I think she now understood my time crunch. "That way." She pointed to her right.

Still trying to catch my breath, I nodded again, able to squeeze out a whispery "thank you" as I spun around and hurried off.

"Feel free to stop by after the service." Her words chased me as I sped off. I nodded again, fully intending to, but I never did.

The sanctuary, occupying the former space of the mall's anchor store, opened before us. I gasped at the enormity of the room, overwhelmed for the third time since our arrival.

I remember no details about the service, only that the music and message were even more than I hoped they would be. Since that time, the founding pastor left. From what I can piece together, his departure was a combination of controversy, dissention, burnout, and disillusionment. Thankfully, there was no misconduct or impropriety on his part. It was just people being the flawed vessels that we are, which caused him to leave.

I persisted in listening to the weekly podcasts, learning to embrace the teaching pastor who replaced him. The new pastor was good, too, but in a different way. I enjoyed his messages and learned directly applicable insight. This, however, was a short-term arrangement, for the new pastor resigned after the board revised his job description. Unwilling to follow this church through another transition, I stopped listening to the podcasts, even though the newest guy was quite good.

More Than 52 Churches

Now we have a chance to visit again. This time, we plan to arrive extra early.

The allure this church once had on me is now gone, but I'm still excited to make a return trip. Contrary to what I once thought, however, I now doubt this could become our church home. The pull is gone, the congregation is too large, and it's not that close to our house.

The rumor is that attendance dropped significantly since our last visit, while other sources claim that's an exaggeration. Soon we'll find out.

As we drive, I pray for our time there, what we will learn, and what God wants to teach us. I know where they're located and drive to the spot. Even so, alarm surges through me when I don't see their sign. My impulse is to flee, but Candy would never stand for that. I must press on.

There is plenty of room in the parking lot, supporting the claim of lost members. However, this time we approached the building from the other direction. The other side of the parking lot could be fuller. From what I can see, it is.

The building boasts signs for the other tenants but not one for the church. *Which entrance do we try?* Then I spot their logo over one set of doors—no name, just a logo. People flow in that direction. We join them.

Last time I picked the farthest entrance and worst place to park. This time I found the best entrance and a convenient place to park. This time our approach is quite different. My anticipation builds.

Inside, people from the first service mingle, some sharing coffee and bagels, others enjoying prolonged conversations. This corridor is wide and easy to navigate. Ahead unfolds the sanctuary, and I don't even need to look for the information booth. What overwhelmed me last time, now unfolds with ease. Am I that different now or has the church changed that much? I suspect the answer lies within me. My perception has changed the most.

At the doors to the sanctuary, a man hands me a paper. I don't remember anyone passing out bulletins last time. This doesn't seem like an usher-and-bulletin type of church. "You'll need this for the service," the guy says with a smile. I wonder why and glance at it. It's labeled "Advent Liturgy." Now I'm really confused. This certainly doesn't seem like a liturgical church.

We move into the sanctuary, a large square room. With in-the-round seating, chairs aligned in sections, 360 degrees around the center stage, there is no apparent front. The few times I've experienced this configuration, the result was satisfying, though not ideal. Sometimes the speaker faces you and other times you see their back. I look around for cameras, suspecting to be able to watch a front-on view on screens. I see no cameras, but there are four screens, configured as a box and suspended over the stage.

The room capacity is too massive to even try to estimate, so I'll simply say it seats thousands. Attendance is sparse when we arrive early. It's about 95 percent full when the service starts.

Sixteen pillars support the beams that in turn support the roof. Each of the pillars is wrapped in evergreen-like garland and strings of white Christmas lights. It gives a festive feel in a smartly understated way. The only other holiday accessory is a display with the five Christmas candles. There is no gaudy glitz or overproduced Christmas display here to assault us. This conforms nicely to the minimalist feel of the entire room: open ceiling painted black, block walls painted beige, and the sixteen pillars. A stained-glass display on one wall is the only artwork. The tables and stations around the stage suggest we'll have communion. The peace of God fills me.

A worship team of seven gathers on the stage, hinting that the service is about to start. As they scatter to their positions, I'm dismayed that most will have their backs to me, though I will have a side view of the worship leader. He also plays guitar. Rounding out the ensemble is another guitarist, a bass guitarist, a drummer (who's sequestered out of view on the opposite side of the stage), a keyboardist (who breaks out an accordion for one song), and two backup vocalists.

We open with part one of the liturgy, "Gathering God's People," followed by the opening song. Their subdued playing lacks the excitement I anticipated. Then they teach us a song, complete with Latin words. Candy knows it, having learned it in Elementary School. It's a simple song, but the timing befuddles me, and the words perplex me. This reminds me of criticism once levied against the Catholic Church for conducting Mass in Latin. The people learned to participate but had no idea what they were saying. So it is with me and this irritating little ditty.

I assume the song, along with the restrained playing and liturgy, is something different they're doing for Advent: changing what is familiar into something with a mystical aura to highlight the significance of the season. I appreciate the intent, but for me it falls short of what I expected and leaves me wanting.

Next is part two of the liturgy, "Responding to God's Presence," with a canticle (responsive reading), lighting the next Advent candle, more singing, and a liturgical prayer, which employs much repetition, apparently for emphasis.

Then we recite the Lord's Prayer in unison, followed by a time of greeting. We have brief interactions with those sitting around us and then, unable to move from our seats, we stand there writhing in awkward isolation.

Following this is "Encountering God's Word," part three of the liturgy. I suspect that for each Sunday in Advent they examine a different gospel account of Jesus's birth. Today we read part of Matthew 1. After reciting a prayer for understanding, we listen to the message.

The teaching is a real treat. The speaker communicates like few others. With an easy-to-listen-to style, he offers a fresh perspective in a most engaging manner. Enthralling is the best word to describe the experience. Though I occasionally hear ministers whose message I really appreciate, this one takes things to a higher level. He artfully draws parallels between the birth of Jesus and the birth of Moses. I'm engaged, inspired, and encouraged.

As he expounds on the text and details the striking parallels between Moses and Jesus, he also throws in some notable one-liners: "Religious people like rules. Jesus was most critical with religious people," "The Bible is more like a family album than a rule book," and "Denominations are involved in verse wars." For a final parallel between Moses and Jesus, he connects the Passover celebration with Communion. "Come to the table, and eat what is free."

People flow forward to partake, using the intinction method: dipping the bread into the juice. With multiple stations to choose from, which present options, some gather in groups around self-serve tables and others approach solitary stands for a private encounter, while the rest go to pairs of people who offer the elements in a more personal manner.

Without intent or discussion, Candy and I veer toward a couple who reverently hold the elements. "The body of Christ, broken for you," smiles the lady as I take the unleavened cracker.

"And for you," I nod.

Moving to her partner, he says, "This is the blood of Christ, shed for you." I nod in silence as I wait for Candy to join me.

We dip our crackers together. "Jesus died for you," I tell her. Then we eat the symbolic meal as we gaze into each other's eyes, mindful of Jesus's awesome love for us. As we do this, music plays and people sing along, with the words displayed overhead. The music is soft and calm, with a holy reverence permeating the place.

The liturgy calls for lighting candles as we sing, but they'll skip this step today. The minister quips something about fire codes and problems last Sunday. People laugh with understanding. I wish I'd been there to witness what happened.

The final part of the liturgy is "Sending God's People." We recite a written prayer and the minister dismisses us.

Candy and I gather our things slowly, hoping for a chance to interact with someone, anyone. To my dismay, all those around us focus on other things. I can't catch anyone's attention. We are invisible. We put on our coats with deliberate slowness and drift toward an exit. Then the woman who served us communion approaches Candy. She introduces herself. Now Candy recognizes her. Their paths occasionally crossed years ago in the city where we used to live and where she still does. She gladly makes an hour-plus drive every Sunday to attend this church. She's done so for years because of the sermons. If today's message is any indication, I understand.

I suspect this Sunday's teaching was typical and the rest of the service was not. While appreciative for the words I heard, I'm dismayed that we didn't experience one of their normal services. Somber music pulls me down, while liturgy pushes me away, both things I need to work on overcoming. It took the message to fully engage me.

On the drive home we share our thoughts. "I loved the teaching," I tell Candy, "but I don't have the energy to try to plug into a large church."

"That's what small groups are for," she says, reminding me what we've discussed before.

"I don't think I even have the energy for that." I pause as I try to process the disconnect of my emotions. "But the message was really, really great."

Takeaway for Leaders: When you're having a nontypical service, how can you best minister to visitors who came to experience one of your normal services?

CHURCH #60: A MISSED OPPORTUNITY

I meet a woman at a writers conference. In addition to being an author, she is also a pastor. She's launching a new church in an underserved downtown urban area. Her dream is a church for people of all ages, races, and backgrounds—a colorful mosaic of folks who seek to grow together in Jesus under the power of the Holy Spirit. She shares more. Her passion draws me in. Her vision inspires me. I want to be part of this great adventure.

I occasionally see her online, reminding me of this church. Being part of this church is not inconceivable, even though the downtown area is about thirty minutes away. I share my excitement over the possibility with Candy. She doesn't see the opportunity I see. Urban church experiences in a rundown area aren't what she wants, but she does agree to visit once.

I go online to find the details. Their website casts a vision for a downtown church, but it also talks about their meetings in a suburb. Details appear for a suburban church service, but not for a downtown one.

In frustration, I fill out the contact form on their website to seek clarity. A couple of weeks later I receive a response, not from my friend, but from her associate. They have not yet started meeting downtown and are presently only gathering in the suburban location. We are welcome to join them. The problem is the suburb is northeast of downtown, while we are southwest. It would take an additional fifteen or so minutes to get there. Forty-five minutes is too far of a drive, even to visit a church one time.

Several months later, I think about this church again. I wonder if their downtown meetings have started. I revisit their website. A picture of the downtown remains, but they have no mention of their downtown vision or meeting there.

I'm disappointed.

I understand that dreams can change, and vision can shift. I assume they've given up on reaching the downtown urban area, just like many other well-intentioned folks. They are now content in the suburbs. Most people are.

Takeaway for Leaders: When vision and dreams change, how do you engage with the people who bought into the original concept?

CHURCH #61: THE WRONG TIME TO VISIT

Based solely on their name, I assume this church is of the same denomination as Church #19 ("A Near Miss"). I enjoyed my time at that church, but I also recall their pastor saying the denomination's member churches vary widely in their beliefs, with most holding a liberal theology. I wonder what I'll encounter at today's destination.

It turns out my speculation is needless.

Their website says they are nondenominational. I'm at the same time disappointed and pleased. I'm disappointed for not being able to broaden my understanding of this denomination, but I am pleased to be able to enjoy a nondenominational experience, which is my preference.

My false assumption about their affiliation reminds me to avoid making wrong conclusions about a church or forming misguided expectations. While this tendency to categorize—that is, to label things—is a natural leaning that aids our understanding, it can cloud our perspective as much as enhance it. The problem is that "nondenominational" is also a label, which can carry false expectations and produce needless assumptions. Furthermore, in reviewing the "Our Beliefs" section of their website, I add the label of *evangelical* and note that it sounds *Baptist*. I've removed one wrong label and replaced it with three new ones: nondenominational, evangelical, and Baptist. I'm no closer to a reasonable understanding of what to expect.

I do know a few other things about them, however, which are more tangible. First, they have two services. I've driven by on many Sunday mornings, noting a parking lot that was three-quarters full for their first service and a packed lot for their second. I also know they are planning on a building project to add space. While the size of a church doesn't impress me and growth can be a misleading indicator, both *can* signal spiritual vitality. I'm intrigued.

Candy is gone this weekend, so I will be on my own. I'm okay visiting a church by myself, but that also gives me the freedom to vacillate. Staying home is a tempting option, one which I consider and reject multiple times. To end my uncertainty, I decide to visit the first service. This is, in part, to give me less time to change my mind but also because I have a lot planned for the rest of the day.

As a result of my volunteer work at a budget program that meets at this church facility during the week, I know where the church is and how long it will take to drive there. I time my departure to arrive ten minutes early. I don't need to.

The parking lot has plenty of space when I arrive. I'm underwhelmed. *Where are all the people?* I walk in with a woman whose husband drops her off by the door. I know her from my volunteer work, but she doesn't recognize me.

We talk a bit anyway. Across the narthex I spot another familiar face from the budget program. I consider going over to talk to her, but I don't. She is by herself and so am I. I'm mindful that confusion or discomfort could result if I approach her alone. Aside from saying "hi" or giving an acknowledging nod, I've never communicated with either of these ladies before.

Other people occupy the narthex, a few in private conversation and others moving about but with no discernable pattern. Without my partner by my side, I feel more exposed and am more uncomfortable than usual when just standing around. I look for someone to talk to—not that I expect to find anyone. The few people I see are all preoccupied. Once again no one notices me.

I turn to the sanctuary, where there are even fewer folks. I stand in the doorway, looking about, giving ample time for someone to approach. No one does. Two guys in the sound booth focus on preparations. Another man stands on the stage. I assume he's part of the worship team. Two people are already sitting, while a third flits about. I smile, looking as approachable as possible. No one sees me.

The hexagon-shaped space is newer construction, open and inviting, though not well-lit and possessing few windows. The six walls give way to six roof sections, which reach up and converge in the center. There are three sections of comfortable looking chairs, angled to face the front. On stage sits a drum kit and several guitars, hinting at a contemporary sound. If there's an organ, I don't see it. Along the back wall sit the readied accessories for communion.

Having held my position and my smile for as long as I can stand to, I meander in to select my seat. Of the two hundred or so options, I head to the second aisle, go up a third of the way and scoot in two spaces. After sitting, I lay my Bible on the chair to my left and put my coat on my right. I'm not saving seats, but with plenty of room, why not spread out? When I realize I could be signaling people to not sit near me, I consolidate my coat and Bible on one chair.

After a few minutes a man comes up and introduces himself. He welcomes me and gives me a bulletin. Then, with a smile, he turns and leaves, just as I open my mouth to speak. I read the entire bulletin—twice. A couple sits directly behind me. Given over 190 other places they could have sat, I take this as an encouraging sign. Twice I turn to interact with them, but they're not interested, offering only the most basic responses and scowling when they do.

Now time for the service to start, it doesn't. Eventually the worship team of seven congregates on stage. The worship leader plays guitar. Helping him is another guitarist, bass guitarist, drummer, and keyboardist. Two ladies round out the ensemble, ready to add backup vocals. There are as many people onstage and in the sound booth as there are sitting down. This low attendance is not at all what I expected.

I anticipate a light pop sound for the music. Instead I'm treated to rock with the hint of an edge. How exciting. The opening strains of their prelude call people into the sanctuary. Our numbers grow to about twenty-five and another ten or so eventually join us. Most of the people are couples in their twenties and thirties, though a few are older. Aside from a baby in the back with her parents, there are no kids or teens. I know there are classes for the kids, but I wonder

More Than 52 Churches

about the teens. Where are they? Do they go to the second service?

The assistant pastor welcomes us and says the senior pastor is out of town. Filling in for him is one of their members, a second-year seminarian. This is not what I hoped for, nor what I want to experience. Maybe I should have stayed home after all. I wonder if their pastor being gone and a student filling in might account for the low attendance, or at least lower than what their parking lot typically suggests.

After an opening prayer, we sing some contemporary songs. With no songbooks, the words project on an overhead screen. It's offset slightly from the stage, but not so much as to be uncomfortable. The first song is a familiar tune but with slightly altered words, which trip me up every time we get to the chorus. Fortunately, I doubt I'm singing loud enough for anyone but God to hear. The second song is likewise familiar, but our rendition lacks the punch and power that I'm used to when David Crowder sings it.

Following these two songs are announcements and an instruction to "greet *everyone* around you." As I shake hands with the guy in front of me, I surprise him when I ask, "How are you?"

With his attention already shifting to the next person to greet, he does a double take. He looks back at me and smiles. "Fine, how are you?"

"Great!"

Before I can respond further, I've lost him again. There will be no conversation, no chance for a connection. I turn to the couple behind me. Although brief, this is our best interaction all morning. I manage to shake hands with a few more people, but fail to make eye contact with those just out of reach. They are not available to see my wave or receive a nod of acknowledgement.

I'm weary of these trivial attempts at greeting, which confront me at too many churches. I want real connection, not people going through the motions: faking friendly when instructed and withdrawing the rest of the time. I'm quite sure this is not what "meeting together" means in Hebrews 10:24–25.

Then we sing two more contemporary songs. Both are familiar—and quite comfortable. We sit down for communion. It is "open to all who believe in Jesus." I'm glad to know this. Too often churches fail to share this important information, leaving me in a quandary about what to do.

They skip the bread. *Curious.* Instead they offer the juice in tiny plastic cups presented on a glistening chrome platter passed up and down the rows. As I reach for mine, I notice the cup is double stacked. I consider taking just the top one with the juice and leaving the bottom one, but it's easier to grab both, so I do.

I now know I *may* participate, but I don't know *when.* Do they drink the cup together, as each person feels led, or do they have some unexplained ritual? I agonize over what to do, so focused on the *when,* that I fail to celebrate the *why.* Then the lady to my right quickly drinks the juice. Seconds later a man a couple of rows up does the same. Relieved to know their process, I'm anxious to follow, lest I call attention to myself should I tarry too long.

I fail to corral my racing mind to focus on God. I can't quiet my heart to consider what Jesus did for us. The harder I try, the tighter anxiety grips me. *God, I am so sorry I can't focus.* Time slips by. As more people partake, my chance to join them grows short. Convinced that God knows my heart and will not hold it against me for not taking time to appropriately acknowledge the ultimate sacrifice of his Son, my Savior, I throw out a desperate prayer. *Thank you, Jesus,* and I drink the juice.

Feeling a bit guilty, yet also relieved, my next question is what to do with the empty container? I glance at it, noticing something trapped between the two cups. Lifting the first one, the mystery item comes into focus. It's a little square communion cracker, the tiniest I've ever seen. Now so much makes sense. They didn't skip the bread. They passed the elements together. That's why one person seemed to drink twice. First they ate the cracker and then they drank the juice. Their motions, especially for the cracker, reminded me of people I've seen in movies doing shots.

I need to eat the cracker, but I'm not doing it like a shot. Smirking, I fish the miniature wafer out from the plastic container. As unobtrusively as possible I slide it into my mouth. With one chomp I demolish it. I swallow, wishing for a chaser of juice.

Today I did communion backward and failed to fully embrace this remembrance of God's gift to me. Even though I merely went through the motions, somehow it seems all right, even good. I envision Father God in Heaven, laughing with his Son over my consternation. Standing at their side, Holy Spirit remains silent but grins broadly. I smile, too, suspecting I gave them a bit of pleasure through my disquiet and my unfilled desire to do communion right. A tear forms. God is so good.

I have little time to consider his goodness, however. The offering follows as soon as they finish passing the communion elements. I already filled out the visitor card and, as instructed, I place it in the offering plate when it passes. The plate is small but able to accommodate cash and checks, but the oversized visitor card does not fit. It hangs a couple of inches over the edge. This will make it hard to contain the donations of those sitting behind me.

With the collection done, our guest preacher stands up. He begins with a prayer. His disjointed speaking—pausing too long midsentence or after each phrase—exposes his uneasiness. I understand. I ache for him. His message is about Zacchaeus, the rich tax collector, as recorded by Doctor Luke in chapter nineteen, verses one through ten. He notes that whenever Jesus encounters a tax collector, the outcome is good. Whenever he encounters a rich man, the outcome is not. With Zacchaeus being both a tax collector and rich, there is tension over what will happen. I question this distinction. Weren't all tax collectors wealthy?

The guy is green. He should be practicing in seminary, not on a congregation. Yes, his introduction shows promise, but his presentation fails to deliver. His points are trivial and only loosely connected. Despite the first three items coming from the text, his fourth does not. Instead it's pulled from an unnamed song that I don't know. He ends with an invitation of sorts, followed with another prayer.

With the Holy Spirit's help, I gain one insight. Hinging on the word "today," I see a parallel between Zacchaeus and the thief on the cross who hangs next to Jesus. In both cases, they make a profession of some kind to Jesus and he pronounces an immediate reward for them of "today," (Luke 19:8–9 and Luke 23:40–43). God's idea of salvation seems so much different than what we've turned it into.

Finished, the speaker sits, and the worship team gets up to play an old hymn, one tweaked to work well with guitars and drums. It's familiar, but out of place with the rest of the service. I wonder if they work an obligatory hymn into each service to keep the traditionalists among them happy.

The assistant pastor returns to give the closing prayer and then the worship team reprises their opening song—the one with different words—to conclude the service. Once again, I stumble over the changed lyrics. At its conclusion, the worship leader abruptly dismisses us.

I stand slowly, trying my best to look friendly and appear approachable. Inside I am, but I wonder what my body language communicates. I often consider this and likely cause more harm than good when I attempt to contort myself into an open posture.

Regardless, no one notices, and no one approaches. With nothing else to do, I amble toward the sanctuary doors, where the guest speaker stands, receiving handshakes and good wishes from the crowd. I, however, don't want to talk to him. I won't lie and tell him he did a good job. And I fear any form of encouragement could come out as backhanded criticism. I can't even share an element of his teaching that I liked, because I didn't like any of it.

I shake his hand in silence. He looks at me with a question forming in his eyes. Then I realize he's a member of this church and doesn't know me. I share my name, and he thanks me for visiting.

I nod and slide into the narthex. No one leaves, but I see no indication of any fellowship time or informal gathering. Not having my bride with me is even more isolating. I feel awkward just standing there. To avoid any more discomfort, I give up. I turn right and hit the main doors. I'm the first to leave.

Driving home, I carry frustration with the threat of tears. I enjoyed the music, and, in an odd way, communion worked for me, but the message caused consternation, and the lack of connection left me empty. If only their senior pastor had been there, I'm sure my experience would have been different.

Then I realize I forgot to pray before the service. That would have made an even bigger difference. *Sorry, Papa. I messed up—big time.*

Takeaway for Leaders: Be careful who you invite to speak at your church. Balance their need to gain experience with attendees' needs to hear a meaningful message.

CHURCH #62: OFF TO A GREAT START

I notice a church sign in front of a school. It's not been there before. I'm quite sure. I'm partial to churches that meet in nontraditional spaces. They are more likely to be nontraditional in their approach to God, being spiritually invigorating and providing a breath of freshness. As a bonus, they don't have the hassle of a building to distract them or the expense of a monthly mortgage payment to weigh down their budget. I have high expectations. Church is at 10 a.m.

It's a new church, a nondenominational church plant, with the congregation that sent them residing several states away. It's curious that an out-of-state church would plant one in an area noted for its religious reputation, with "a church on every corner." Even so, they did just that.

The day is mild and sunny. A light breeze presents the perfect combination of weather, belying the norm for an August day in southwest Michigan. We arrive ten minutes early. The parking lot is about half full. A man stands along the walk at the parking lot's edge. He doesn't need to direct us to the entrance because there is only one set of doors. A most gregarious fellow, he is there to greet us. What a wonderful welcome to church. With his broad smile and easy banter, we immediately feel at ease. His laidback embrace lets me know our experience here will be a good one.

At the door stands another man. He sports a red T-shirt, asking the question: "How can I serve you?" With an engaging smile, he welcomes us, opening the door with a gracious flourish. The friendly reception of these two men is infectious. I can't wait to experience church here.

Our greeting isn't over. Just inside stand a couple, also wearing red T-shirts. They further welcome us. We exchange names and they repeat ours, making a pointed effort to remember them. Excited to see us, we talk a bit. Among other things, they tell us about the coffee and snacks that await us inside. Having never received such a grand welcome when visiting a church, we move into the meeting space.

The room is curious, more resembling a church than a school. It is a modern space, about square, with a permanent stage in one corner. The flat floor hints that this is an all-purpose room, albeit now nicely carpeted and smartly finished. An out-of-place scoreboard hangs high on one wall, but there's no hint that the space would work for a sporting event.

Chairs, arrayed in three sections, face the stage, offering enough room for about two hundred. A music video plays, providing background sound and a nice visual on the screen overhead. After a couple of minutes, the video stops and a countdown timer appears, starting at five minutes. My excitement mounts.

With only seconds remaining in the countdown, the worship team scrambles to the stage. The guitar player barely makes it in time, but to their credit, they launch into song when the timer hits zero. The worship leader plays keyboard, flanked by a guitarist and backup vocalist. The drummer sits behind them, along with a bass guitarist. With a rock sound, we sing two songs in the opening set.

The associate pastor comes up and welcomes us. He asks first-time visitors to raise their hands. Quite a few do, including the couple sitting next to us. With few empty seats, attendance must approach two hundred, quite remarkable for a new church during the month of August. I suspect a huge jump in the fall.

He tells us to greet those around us. This period of welcome is neither stellar nor lame, but it is pleasant, despite a lack of time for meaningful connection. Then he announces the offering, stressing that it's only for regular attendees, not visitors. They don't use offering plates but velvet bags with wooden handles. They are awkward for me to pass. As the offering bags work their way down the rows and across the aisles, the associate pastor gives some announcements.

The church is only four months old, having launched on Easter. In a few weeks they will have a "gathering with the pastors" for new people who want to learn more about the church. He also plugs small groups, "E-3 Groups," which stands for Encounter, Embrace, and Engage. Taking August off, the groups will resume in September. After a few other announcements, he reads selected passages from Psalms.

After this respite, the worship team leads us in four more

songs. All are contemporary, but none are familiar. The senior pastor, who is taking a break from teaching in the month of August, dismisses the children for their own activities. Then he introduces today's guest speaker.

He is the founding pastor from the church that sent this team to plant a church. He opens by giving some background. When they decided to plant a church, they considered several possibilities across the United States but kept coming back to this region, even though there didn't seem to be a need.

Despite the many churches in the vicinity, this area is "over-Bibled and under-Jesused." Given this church's rapid numeric growth and the excitement surrounding their gathering, I think they're right in their assessment of a need to plant a church in this locale.

Today he will speak from Philippians chapter three. Ushers pass out Bibles to anyone who doesn't have one and would like one. I'm not sure if this is just for the service or to keep. The Bibles are English Standard Version (ESV). In a bit of irony, however, the pastor uses the more popular NIV for his discourse.

"We need to attack the lie that you can have it all," he says. "It's not possible. Something needs to give." Although most engaging, I struggle to catch all the nuances in his rapid-fire delivery.

The apostle Paul was willing to lose everything so he could gain Jesus. "What are you willing to lose?" He reminds us of the parables of the hidden treasure and the pearl in Matthew 13:44–46, where a man and a merchant are both willing to give up everything for one great treasure. Then he quotes Socrates: "An unexamined life is not worth living."

He concludes his message with a prayer, followed by a time of introspection, reminiscent of an altar call, sans "with every head bowed" and an invitation to come forward. "Is Jesus the point in your life?" he asks.

The worship band comes up for a closing number and then the associate pastor dismisses us with a benediction. The staff is available up front for anyone who wants prayer.

Before I can talk to the visitors sitting next to me, they scoot out. During the greeting time, I learned the guy behind me shares my first name. I'd like to talk more to my namesake, but he is already engaged in another conversation, as are the folks who sat in front of us. With no one to talk to, we make our way out.

In the lobby stand the couple who greeted us when we arrived. They remember our names and conversation. They wish us a good day and invite us back.

This church is off to a great start. They are already making a difference in the community and poised to make an even greater impact in the future. Their numeric growth is obvious and the potential for spiritual growth is present. They are meeting an unmet need in what some would call an already over-churched area.

Takeaway for Everyone: To effectively embrace visitors, it's essential to make a great first impression. This starts before they enter the sanctuary, even before they enter the building.

CHURCH #63: WE DON'T NEED NO SERMON

A few months ago, my wife started a new job. One of her coworkers goes to a church near the one we normally attend. "I'd like to visit it sometime," she says, catching me off guard. With a non-church sounding name, I'm intrigued.

Her openness to go there surprises me. "Are you looking to change churches?"

"I just want to visit once," she says with a decided tone. "Besides, *you* need a break from our church."

She is right. I so need a break. I long for a respite from their too-long, too-pointless sermons. Once again, I find myself enduring the church service so I can enjoy church camaraderie afterward.

The music at our current church is okay. I persist in it as an act of worship. I sing and occasionally lift my hands to honor God, but not because I necessarily like the selections or the playing. I believe I honor God with my physical act of worship, even though my mind is seldom engaged. I do it for him, not because I feel like it.

Their hour-long sermons, however, seem pointless. Our teaching elder is a gifted scholar with an occasional quirk in his delivery when he diverges from his notes. My beef is that he only teaches. He gives no application. It's an info dump, sans meaningful spiritual relevance. At best it's an entertaining lecture. I leave each Sunday no closer to God than when I arrived. I head home with no challenge to live differently or conviction to change or correct anything.

His messages tell me about the Bible, but his words don't draw me to God. "Knowledge puffs up," Paul writes to the church in Corinth (1 Corinthians 8:1). I fear we are a puffy church, self-satisfied over the depth of our Bible knowledge.

Mostly he reminds me of what I already know. More pointedly, his ultra-conservative theology often chafes at my soul. Too often I anticipate where he is headed and whisper emphatically, "No, no, no!"

Despite my silent warning, he goes there anyway. He ends up where I think he shouldn't, espousing a view of God I don't see much support for in the Bible as much as emanating from blindly following accepted fundamental principles. I fear I will one day protest too loudly.

"You've had a bad attitude for the past two weeks," my wife reminds me.

She's right, of course. On our drive to church the past few weeks I sigh and sometimes murmur that I can't bear the thought of sitting through another sermon. Then we pray. And later I do what I don't want to do: listen to another download of Bible knowledge without a greater purpose. A break from this will be good.

As we drive to visit the church Candy's coworker attends, I'm so glad for a reprieve from ours and the pointless lecture. Even so, I will miss seeing the people there. A pang of guilt stabs my heart. It's like I'm cheating on my church by seeing another one. I feel unfaithful. I am unworthy of their friendship.

We could drive past our church to get to this one, but I choose a different route. We pull into the parking lot to see a typical-looking church building, despite their nonconventional name. I expected something different. The parking lot appears mostly full, and I pull into an open spot next to the dumpster. As we walk to the building, I see two and then four spots reserved for visitors. All are empty.

We can easily tell where to enter the building, but once inside we don't know where to go. A few people cautiously greet us. They know we aren't regulars, but at the same time they aren't sure if we've visited before or if this might be our first time. I ask one of them where the sanctuary is. She uses her head to point us in the right direction, which is opposite of what I assumed. We weave our way through the people, all engaged in conversation with friends—and too busy to notice us.

Instead of standing around and looking pathetic, we open the closed doors of the sanctuary. It's an octagon-shaped space with a high sloped ceiling converging in the center. Block walls and impressive wooden beams give an open feel. Oscillating fans mounted on the walls tell me they lack air conditioning. Today that doesn't matter. Despite warm weather for this time of year, we're still within winter's final grasp.

With padded pews arranged in four sections, the room accommodates three to four hundred. "Pick any place you want," I whisper to Candy, "but please not too far toward the front." Instead of moving, she stops to scan the room. Off to the side, she spots her coworker and waves. He beckons us. His face beams.

"I'm so glad you're here," he smiles. He is truly overjoyed to see us. He introduces us to some friends and invites us to sit with his family in their usual spot, even though they aren't yet here. "Sharon will be so surprised to see you." A gracious man, we feel most welcomed. Then he excuses himself and joins the worship team gathering on the stage.

As predicted, his wife is indeed surprised to see us. She is as excited as he. They both make us feel so welcomed, so embraced, so loved. It's an ability I don't have, and I've seldom seen people who wield this skill of hospitality so adeptly as this couple. Though everyone in a church can, and should, greet visitors, some people have a real gift for it.

We learn that this is "Faith Promise Sunday," so they won't have a sermon. The lack of a sermon overjoys me, yet I wonder, what will fill the time? Is this their annual budget drive? We once visited a church when they did this (Church #32, "Commitment Sunday and Celebration"), securing pledges for the upcoming year. They even brought in a heavy hitter to lead the fund drive and maximize the pledges. Though it lacked an emotion-laden plea, I still squirmed a time or two. Will today be like that? I'll need to wait to find out because we have an opening song set first.

A contemporary team leads us in song: the song leader on guitar, two female backup vocals, bass guitar, keys, drums, and Candy's coworker on percussion. They have a light rock sound, though it's obvious the lead guitarist is holding back—way back. Some of the songs are new to us, but even the familiar ones move at a slower pace than I like, so I struggle to sing along. The backup vocalists occasionally raise their hands in praise, but no one else does in the congregation of about one hundred. (I see only adults, so the kids must be in their own program.) Not wanting to confront their practices, I clasp my hands behind my back to prevent any spontaneous wayward movement. Besides, I don't want to call attention to myself.

Then one of their three pastors explains Faith Promise Sunday, an event they've been moving toward for the past couple of weeks. This is for missions, not their general fund. Distinguishing it from a tithe, this is an above-and-beyond commitment to support missions work. Alluding ever so briefly to 2 Corinthians 8 and 9, he gives biblical precedence for setting aside money each week to support those who do missionary work. By asking for a faith pledge they will be able to let each of the six groups they support know how much money they plan to give them for the year. Ushers pass offering plates to collect the pledges.

With this as a backdrop, they spend the next forty-five minutes or so explaining each of these ministries. They start with three local ones. The first is an after-school program with a structured time for homework, tutoring, literacy, recreation, and spiritual expression. It recently relocated to this facility. For the first time, its two staff members can receive a paycheck. The second local ministry is an urban church, which also just relocated. They now have more space, at a lower cost, for their growing ministry. The third is a husband-wife team with Youth for Christ. Not having local connections, they struggle to raise support.

For the three non-local missions, the first is in the US, a couple of states away. It's a Christian youth home, which struggled for a while when they refused to capitulate to their state's insistence that they do not mention faith or God.

Having found a workaround solution, their program is again full. The church also sends mission teams there to help. Next is a program in the UK, part of a global organization that works with schools, community projects, businesses, and churches to repurpose churches with a focus on mission, discipleship, and study. Rounding out the six is a missionary couple covertly working in a Muslim country, one closed to missionaries. Theirs is a solitary effort, with no local community support or Christian connections. They struggle emotionally.

Lay members of the missions committee come up to pray for these organizations and people. Then they announce the pledge total: $44,900. The congregation celebrates this generous commitment. We close with another song set, this one much shorter. The associate pastor dismisses us with little fanfare.

"We're sorry you didn't get to hear a sermon," we hear more than once.

I'm not sorry at all. I heard what I needed. The work of God's people to share his love, both locally and around the world, fed my soul. I find encouragement from a church that treats missions seriously and not as a minor add-on to a normally cash-strapped budget.

As far as church services go, this was one of the best I've experienced in months.

As a bonus, our friends invite us to their house for a Sunday meal. It is so good—and so right—to spend time with other followers of Jesus in intentional community.

Takeaway for Leaders: Make missions a priority, not an ancillary afterthought.

CHURCH #64: IS BIGGER ALWAYS BETTER?

It's been three months since visiting the last church. We've slipped back into the routine of our own church, yet my unrest over going there remains strong.

"Do you want to go to a different church today?" My bride's words surprise me. She just crawled out of bed and, though awake, she seldom talks to me for the first hour or so each morning. Her unusual behavior grabs my attention.

"Where?"

She tells me the name. I'm familiar with it: a nontypical, nondenominational church with a good amount of positive local buzz. It's a couple of towns away but not that far of a drive. I'm not interested in going, but I don't say so. "Why?"

"I'm curious. I drive by it all the time. Also, we know three couples who go there." She lists them.

I've been up for a few hours, moving through my Sunday morning routine of writing, exercise, and Bible study. Well, that's my routine for every morning, but on

Sunday I write next week's blog posts about the Bible and spirituality, a fitting pre-church focus.

I'm open for a break, any break. Yet I hesitate. Already I feel a pang over not seeing my friends at church. I'm also miffed at her springing this on me at the last minute, or what seems the last minute. Had I known last night, I would have adjusted my morning schedule so I could better accommodate visiting this church.

"Yes," I say after a too-long pause, "but how about some other Sunday?"

Her silence tells me "No."

"Do you know what time their services are?"

"Nine and eleven."

Ah, she'd been thinking about this for a while. "I wish you would have told me sooner. You know I struggle with spur-of-the-moment changes." If I drop everything and shower, we could barely make the 9:00 a.m. service. The 11:00 a.m. service, however, will give me an extra thirty minutes. "Nine is out. We can do eleven."

She nods her agreement.

"How long will it take to get there?"

"Thirty minutes will give us enough time."

Then I remember. "Today is Mother's Day. Let's not go on a special Sunday." We recount the last two Mother's Days, both visiting churches (Church #5, "Catholics are Christians Too" and Church #56, "The Reboot"). Those experiences weren't bad, but their special focus of the day was distracting. Then Candy reminds me of the church we visited on Father's Day (Church #10, "A Special Father's Day Message"). Agonizing best describes that experience. I shudder at the recollection. But I suspect any Sunday would have been a rough time to visit that church.

She dismisses my concern, and I acquiesce to her suggestion.

Several years ago, a friend who attends church there encouraged me to listen to podcasts of their sermons. Excited for the opportunity, I downloaded the most recent message and listened to it on my iPod a few days later.

The minister was an engaging teacher, but his topic was most difficult: child pornography. I struggled as I listened, glad for the privacy my earbuds offered. As I recall, he talked about a documentary on this despicable evil. What I remember too vividly was his description of child pornographers shooting one scene. His details were not explicit, but the situation he depicted vexed me so much that I became ill. The memory of what he described torments me to this day. That was the only podcast I listened to from this church.

I don't know the name of that minister or if he's still there, but the image of this deplorable scene is seared into my mind and firmly associated with this church. Hence, I'm apprehensive about going there.

We chat on the drive there, forgetting to pray until we spot their building, "God, be with us at church," I say in haste. "Amen."

Two young women, stationed at the entrance to the parking lot, smile and wave as we drive past. What a nice greeting. We pull into the lot, but there is no one to direct traffic. Some people are still leaving from the first service. I see no open spots. I make a quick turn away from the building and head for what I hope will be available parking spaces.

We park with ease and follow the flow of people to entrance #2. Greeters hold the doors open, giving us inviting smiles and a brochure as we walk into the facility. A large open area, reminiscent of Church #51 ("The Megachurch: A Grand and Welcoming Experience"), steals my breath. People move in all directions toward a myriad of options, with no clear flow pointing us to the sanctuary. My head bobbles, trying in vain to determine the correct direction to head.

I spot a lady sporting a name tag and wearing a T-shirt that suggests she's a greeter. Her broad smile beckons me. There's no point in pretending we know what we're doing.

"This is overwhelming," I tell her. "Which way do we go?"

"That depends what you're looking for," she says with a playful jab.

"For the service," I clarify, trying to smile and not look like an ogre.

She points to her right, and I nod.

"Coffee?" Candy asks.

"Sure," she smiles and points in the opposite direction. "And the bathrooms are back there," she gestures to the vast space behind her.

"That's everything we need to know." I thank her for her assistance and turn toward the sanctuary, but Candy is already heading for the coffee. I fall in behind her. There are no baristas to make a custom concoction, but there is an array of air pots with a nice range of self-serve options. She makes her selection and stirs in the desired additives. Now we can go sit down.

The worship space is square, with the stage in the center of the room, reminding us of Church #59 ("Big, Yet Compelling"), though not as huge. It seats a thousand or so. It's hard to estimate, having just walked in. I could easily be off by 50 percent. With seating in the round, I try to make a split-second decision of the optimum place to sit. It's pointless, so we head to some empty chairs. While my goal is to sit quickly and not call attention to myself, Candy usually takes a more deliberate approach to seat selection.

The sound booth is opposite us and a digital clock, I assume to keep the minister on schedule, reveals it's 11:00. It's time to start, yet nothing happens. The worship team gathers. We spot one of our friends on bass. I count eight on the team: two lead vocalists also on guitars, two backup vocalists, a keyboardist, a drummer, a third guitarist, and our friend on bass guitar.

About five minutes late, with the place now packed, the music swells. With a pleasing rock vibe, they launch into the first song. The worship team faces each other, which means those closest have their backs to us. They need to do this to get their cues from their leader. It's disconcerting, but it makes their playing less of a performance and more like the worship service it's supposed to be.

The words to this unfamiliar song appear on four screens, connected to form a box suspended over the stage. The angle is too sharp to work well with my bifocals, and I eventually give up trying to sing along, which for me is more akin to mouthing the words, since I don't know the tune and the timing is irregular. The second song is unfamiliar too. I fight an uncomfortable self-consciousness for standing there mute while most others are engaged in spirited worship, swaying to the rhythm and raising their hands in praise.

I try to focus on the words as they're sung, so I can at least worship God in my mind and spirit. I think I've heard the third song before, yet not enough that I can sing along. Eventually I pick up the chorus: "The Resurrected King is resurrecting me." Thank you, Jesus. (I later discover online that we were singing "Resurrecting" by Elevation Worship.)

Not only is today Mother's Day, it's also Ascension Sunday. I expect a focus on moms and wonder if Jesus's ascension into Heaven will receive any mention at all. Since Jesus returned to Heaven forty days after he resurrected from the dead, that makes the actual day last Thursday, known as Ascension Thursday. For convenience sake, the church calendar moves the acknowledgement to the Sunday after, Ascension Sunday. Most churches I've attended skip this completely, yet some mention it in passing. Today, singing about Jesus's resurrection is the closest we will get to acknowledging his ascension.

The opening song set concludes and moves into a video about a local homeless outreach, but I miss the explanation as to why they play it. Announcements follow the video and then a prayer for moms. With a focus on celebrating motherhood, the prayer also admits this day is difficult for some, covering those who want to be moms and can't, as well as those who were moms and no longer are. The concluding "Amen" wraps up our salute to moms.

Next they do eight baby dedications, striking the right balance between the dedication and celebrating the child, without dragging it into a too-long ceremony. The parents make their pledge to take the lead in raising their kids, then the families and friends add their support, and finally the entire congregation stands to acknowledge their role.

Now we return to their regular schedule.

Since we're already standing, the greeting time follows. Most people engage with one another. However, only one person gives us any attention, and no one near us seems approachable. Candy asks me the icebreaker questions posited on the screens, then I reciprocate. We work through all the suggested questions, yet the time grinds on. After visiting so many churches we're used to the awkwardness of most mid-service greetings, yet they remain agonizing.

In the middle of a series titled "Heroes," this church is examining the heroes of faith as summarized in Hebrews 11. Today we address Abel, who gave a better offering to God than his brother, Cain, Genesis 4:1–7.

"How are we handling our resources?" the pastor asks. Cain gave *some* of his produce to God—not the first, not the best, and not extravagantly—just some. Abel gave the *best* of what he had. And he received God's favor.

"What does it mean to have God's favor?" Our leader guides us to 2 Corinthians 9:6–10 about sowing generously and being a cheerful giver. The Mother's Day message on Abel morphs into a sermon about giving. "Joyful generosity," says the minister, "produces generous blessing." Then he clarifies that the blessing may not be financial. He shares two recent examples from their church family, in which a commitment to give to God, despite hardship, resulted in financial blessing. Apparently he didn't have any examples of non-financial blessings to share.

"Cain gives because he is religious. It's a transaction." Instead, God wants relationship and isn't so interested in us "doing stuff," he explains.

At this point he slides into an altar call of sorts, but instead of coming forward, people should make a note of their decision on the connection card or go to the "Getting Started" area after the service. He drones on, and I soon tune him out, conditioned to do so a long time ago during a five-year stint at an ultraconservative Baptist church. I shudder at the memory.

Next they take the offering, a traditional passing of the plates in this otherwise not-so-traditional setting. Guests are exempt from giving. A closing song concludes the service.

We chat briefly with our bass-playing friend, and then he heads off to spend time with his mom. Not spotting any of our other friends and with no one approaching us or appearing approachable, we head out.

On the way home we debrief. "It was a nice break," I tell Candy. "The music was definitely better than we're used to." The sermon also gives me something to think about. In addition to the teaching about the Bible (which we normally have), I also received encouragement and application (which we normally don't have).

Candy agrees about the music. "But I wouldn't want a steady diet of it." That ends our discussion.

Aside from the people assigned to welcome our arrival and our friend we talked to afterward, we only had the briefest interaction with one other person, which happened during the obligatory greeting time.

As a big church, they offer excellence in their teaching and music, with an array of programs and service opportunities. However, they struggle to offer community and connection. Such is the case in most large churches.

I leave spiritually filled and emotionally hungry.

Takeaway for Leaders: What can you do to foster community and connection at your church?

CHURCH #65: SHORT OF MEETING EXPECTATIONS

Our home church canceled today's Sunday service because everyone (except us) is off at church camp, a weeklong community experience on the shore of Lake Michigan. While many at church dislike camping, they so treasure the extended time with church family that they go anyway. It's a highly anticipated annual event, the highlight of the year.

Candy and I are not there, however. For one, neither of us are campers, not even close. Second, my work schedule and writing demands make taking a week off impossible. Even with much planning, one day off is hard for me to manage with any degree of success. Lastly, the time when everyone else arranged for campers, Candy was embroiled in an intense season at her job that took every waking minute of her time and much of mine.

The result is that we are not at church camp and have a Sunday free.

I'm glad for the reprieve. I need it. Candy doesn't voice

it, but I'm sure she realizes I need a break from the tedious routine of our regular church service. I have a list of churches to visit and have longed to experience this one for over a year. I met one of their staff at a speakers conference. As we talked about her church and their belief in the present-day power of the Holy Spirit, that same Holy Spirit nudged me to visit.

"It won't be soon," I told her, "but it will happen."

"Let me know when," she said, "so I can look for you."

I agreed, anticipating that day, not knowing it would take thirteen months. With this opening in our Sunday schedule, I email her, unsure if she'll remember me. To my delight, she does.

I fill Candy in on the details. "Their service is at ten, and it will take twenty-three minutes to drive there. I'd like to leave at 9:30."

She agrees.

As I move through my Sunday morning, I realize a 9:30 departure won't be soon enough. First, it's unlikely we will leave at that time. Second, we need a cushion in case we have trouble finding the church and to park our car and find our way inside. Third, my goal when visiting churches is to arrive ten minutes early. This allows time for some pre-church interaction but not too much time in case there is none.

When I suggest 9:20 to Candy, she glares. And she shakes off a compromise of 9:25. "You should have told me sooner. I'm on track for 9:30. I don't know if I can be ready before then."

At 9:37 we leave the house. I'm frustrated. As I drive, I pray for our time at this church. I'm still not sure what the Holy Spirit has in mind. My prayer is short and direct.

"Lord, may we learn what you would have us to learn and share what you would have us to share. Amen."

We encounter road construction on the way, which slows us down some but not too much. Our GPS says we'll arrive at 9:57 and then updates our ETA to 9:58. The church sits in a residential area. It's a tired-looking, older facility, a bit on the dreary side, but I don't have time to consider it much as I round the block looking for the parking lot.

We slide into an open space and walk with intention to the entrance. A few others arrive with us. I guess we will be fashionably late together. A woman with a walker lurches forward. If we give her patient passage, the delay will be interminable. If we rush past her, we might still make it by ten. What Would Jesus Do? I shake off that consideration as I scoot around her. Candy follows.

Inside is a bustle of activity, which beckons us to the right, yet I spot a quiet, darkened sanctuary to my left. A greeter of sorts glides up to us to provide an overview of our options. Candy decides to snag a cup of coffee, leaving me alone to wallow in discomfort. When she rejoins me, we head toward the sanctuary and my friend warmly greets us.

Relieved to see a familiar face, I introduce her to Candy and then mutter my despair over cutting the time too close. It's exactly 10:00. She dismisses my distress with a nonchalant wave. "We don't start on time here," she says with a smile. As proof she gestures to the throng still behind us.

I follow Candy into the sanctuary. She bypasses many viable places to sit as she moves too far forward for my comfort. Although sitting toward the front results in fewer distractions, it also makes observation of the congregation more difficult. It's a challenge to balance engagement with examination when visiting churches, and I'm not sure which one the Holy Spirit wants me to focus on today.

Room-darkening shades cover the few windows in the space, and the lights are low. I'm not sure if I like the subdued, almost mystical, vibe or not. The room is about as wide as it is deep, with two hundred chairs, which might be 40 to 50 percent occupied. I expected a bigger sanctuary with more people, but it's mid-August. Church attendance typically ebbs to its low point of the year during late summer.

A worship team of five opens the service. It's a contemporary assembly with the leader on guitar. Joining him are a backup guitarist, bass guitarist, someone on keys, and another on drums. Their sound borders on grunge. Without much coaxing, I envision them cutting loose. They remain restrained, however, suitable for a church service but disappointing for me.

With words displayed overhead, we sing a contemporary song that is new to me and then another and another, four that I have never heard and most of which I struggle to even mouth the words. "Sing a new song," the Bible says repeatedly (Psalm 33:3, 96:1, 98:1, 144:9, and 149:1, as well as Isaiah 42:10.). I try to shove aside my discomfort with the acknowledgement that the Bible never says to give God the old songs we know and like.

The chorus of one song starts to click with me, and I sing along—more or less. One phrase grabs my attention: "we are defiant in your name." (A later search online reveals we sang "More than Conquerors" by Rend Collective.) Self-described as spiritually militant, this line connects with me. I give it to God as my new song.

As we sing, one woman dances worshipfully off to the

right and several more join her with flags on both sides of the stage. Easels of artwork flank each side as well, yet I see no one working on art during worship. A couple of people raise their hands as they sing, but they are so few that I don't want to call attention to myself by joining them, despite a gentle Holy Spirit nudge to do so. Our numbers continue to grow, and by the end of the fourth song I estimate the place is about 60 percent full. Most seem to be older generations without many Gen-Xers or Millennials.

Millennials are supposed to be more open to spiritual things, and my expectation was that I would see them at this church, which is more open to spirituality through the presence and power of the Holy Spirit. I don't see any millennials. I suppose their openness to spirituality doesn't make them equally open to a spiritual experience in a church building, or they just aren't aware of this church.

I fully suspect these spiritually-open Millennials are hanging out elsewhere in nontraditional settings and times. I want to be with them. I also know that not all that is spiritual is good, so I pray they're drawn toward a biblical, Jesus-focused spirituality and not one that runs counter to it.

After a half hour, the music winds down and gives way to the greeting time. This church does better than most in making this awkward time feel not so awkward for visitors. Many give us a sincere welcome, sharing their names and asking ours. They are genuinely interested. With gentle probing they learn about us without prying: "Are you new to the area?" asks one. "Where do you live?" inquires another. "Is this your first time here?" queries a third. "Are you looking for a new church?" And so on.

A countdown display measures the time allotted for greeting. I don't know where it started, but I notice it during a lull in conversation when it says 45 . . . 44 . . . 43 . . . Then my friend comes up and welcomes us again. We're nicely engaged in conversation when someone taps her shoulder and points to the screen. The counter has hit zero and the screen is now blank. My friend is supposed to give announcements, intended to start when the timer hit zero. She scurries off to her assignment.

She gains the attention of the crowd and corrals our disparate conversations. We sit down, but I only half listen. I want to continue our conversation, but we can't. After the announcements, a prayer follows, and they ask first-time visitors to raise their hands. I don't like calling attention to myself this way and grouse at the thought of it. I don't want to play along, but I always do, albeit without much enthusiasm. Even so, I'm relieved we don't need to stand and introduce ourselves, as at Church #20 ("Different Language, Same God").

Someone hands me a card, which I accept, hoping this will end the attention I feel foisted upon me. Thankfully it does. The card invites us to stop by the welcome center after the service for a gift.

The minister stands to give us his message, based on Luke 1:5–25. He talks about living expectantly. Imagine waking up each morning and asking God, "Daddy, what are we going to do today?" What a grand way to live life, but few people do. Instead of living expectantly, we live with expectations, which are bound to disappoint us. I certainly had my expectations about this church, its size, its attendees, and my experience here. I'm sad to admit that today my expectations overshadowed my expectancy.

He wraps up with his prescription for how to live expectantly. The worship team reassembles, playing softly as he gives a call to action. I'm not really listening to what he says, only enough to know that it's not a typical altar call. After the closing song, they move into prayer time, the third part of the service.

Prayer teams come forward in pairs, while most of the congregation files out into the lobby. A few linger for their own time of sharing and praying. Some go forward to meet with the waiting prayer teams. Gentle music plays to produce a safe and holy place.

"Do you want prayer for your knee?" I ask my bride.

"No, you can pray for it at home."

That wasn't the response I expected—or wanted. I long to tarry, but I know Candy does not. I hand her the gift card, which she accepts with an eager smile.

"Meet me in back when you're done," she says, smartly granting me space without subjecting me to her eagerness to leave.

I sit as I try to formulate a reason to go up for prayer. Each thought seems trivial. I consider simply asking a prayer team if God might give them a word to share with me. At the same time, I don't know if they would be comfortable handling such a request. I certainly don't want to put them on the spot or make them uneasy. It's one thing to pray for people in reaction to their request and quite another to proactively listen to what God would give you to share with them.

I've done both, the first with ease and the second with trepidation, fearing that I might not hear correctly or in my anxiety to respond, I might mistake my nervous thoughts for Holy Spirit insight.

Instead of going forward, I sit, basking in God's presence. He asks me gentle questions, which I jot down for further contemplation. Even so, I'm sad. It's been a couple of years since I've been to a church that had time for prayer at the conclusion of each service. At one time I would have been on one of the prayer teams, listening, praying, hugging, and sometimes healing. That seems a lifetime ago. I so miss it. A deep longing emerges. I want to be at a church that allows the laity to minister to one another, not relegating us to passive pew sitting.

My friend is half of one of the prayer teams. She and her partner stay busy praying for others. If they experience a lull, I will go up to talk, open for whatever prayers they will offer or words they might share. I don't have a chance. They steadily move from one person to the next, without a break. What they're doing is more important than what I'm contemplating. I head out to find my bride.

Candy stands at the welcome center, engaged in conversation. The gift was a coffee cup, which she passed on accepting because we already have too many. I catch the end of their conversation, and we turn to leave. One person welcomes us and adds, "Hope to see you next week."

I know he won't, but I don't say so. Instead I nod to acknowledge I heard him and say, "Thank you." I know it's an awkward response, but it's the best I've come up with so that I don't give them false hope or be rude by saying we won't be back.

As we drive home, I'm deep in contemplation, but Candy's thinking about eating, which is usually *my* post-church priority. We talk a bit about the prayer time, me with nostalgic longing and her contrasting it to the church we once attended. There they played music loudly during the prayer time, so intense that we struggled to hear and be heard. Despite our numerous pleas, they never turned the music down. Leadership claimed loud music was most conducive to post-church interaction and the prayer team needed to deal with it. "They do their prayer time right," I say. "This is how it should be done."

Candy agrees.

"The sermon wasn't great, but God gave me a lot to think about," I add. "It will take me a while to process it."

"I didn't like it," she responds. I know my spouse well enough to know she's done talking about church. We go to Burger King for lunch.

Takeaway for Leaders: Provide intentional opportunities for the laity to minister to one another through prayer.

CHURCH #66: GIFTS OF THE SPIRIT

Valued friends invite us to visit a church they've been going to for about six months. This surprises me: not the invitation part but that they're going to an organized church and not the house church they've been involved with for several years. They now attend both, interweaving their participation as their schedule permits.

"They operate in the gifts of the Spirit," my friend says. The chance to see our friends—who we don't see often enough because we live an hour apart—is all the incentive I need. The fact that this day promises to start with a Holy Spirit experience shines as a bonus.

My background is not charismatic, but I relish the opportunity to experience Holy Spirit power and bask in his presence. Our own church portends to embrace the Holy Spirit, but how they conduct their services leaves little room for him to act. Our worship experiences focus on Jesus and his Father. They mention the Holy Spirit but keep him at a safe distance. This, incidentally, was how I experienced church most of my life. And frankly, it wearies me. I want a Trinitarian experience, the whole package, not two out of three.

The Holy Spirit isn't much of a factor in my typical worship experience at our church, but he is a daily factor in my life—though not as much as I'd like. It's harder to embrace him when I'm not surrounded by a community of like-minded faith seekers. I want to be part of a community who operates in the gifts of the Spirit. I *must* be in such a community, but I'm not.

I'm hungry for God. I'm thirsty for more. I can hardly wait for Sunday, counting down the days, which is a good thing since this attitude of church anticipation is now mostly missing from my normal reality.

I check out the church's website. It's fresh. They just rebranded themselves with a new name to better reflect their Holy Spirit focus, but it looks like many websites for any one of today's churches. It views and reads like most seeker-friendly fundamental churches. One bullet point, however, in the "What we believe" section, hints at what we'll experience. It mentions the baptism of the Holy Spirit, speaking in tongues, the gifts of the spirit, and supernatural manifestations. I'm terrified and excited at the same time. I expect God will stretch me, and I welcome what is to come, even though I will surely squirm.

With only a few days to wait, my friend emails me with bad news: Their pastor won't be there on Sunday. My being deflates, but my resolve doesn't. Surely this church, which operates in the gifts of the Spirit, can function just fine without a minister. At least, they should.

My friend gives me an out if I want it, but I don't take it. "Let's proceed as planned." Crisis averted.

More Than 52 Churches

I awake Sunday morning to the promise of unseasonably warm temperatures by midday. But, still in the winter season, it's below freezing at daybreak. A bit of overnight snow and ice coat the roads. This should tell me to leave a bit earlier than planned, but I don't heed the warning.

As we leave home a cheerful sun brightens our journey, an hour-long trek of mostly highway driving, but the roads to reach the highway still retain a bit of winter. I skip taking the shortest route and opt for the more-traveled path. This will add about five minutes to our trip, but having padded it by fifteen, we should still arrive ten minutes early.

We ask God for safe travels and for his blessing on our time at church. We added this practice of a pre-church prayer a few years ago when we began *52 Churches*. I know it's essential, but it's hard to keep the words fresh week after week. So it is today. Does God at least appreciate that we tried?

You'd think I'd be used to visiting churches by now. I'm not. Apprehension over the unknown roils in my gut. A dozen worries assault my mind. It would be easy to turn around and head for our church, the one that's known, the one that talks Holy Spirit even though it does little to back up their claim. Instead, I push on. Regardless of what happens at church, we'll have the afternoon with friends—good friends—to look forward to. I focus on that.

The church meets in a public high school, a fact I appreciate. A temporary banner points us in the right direction, but once we reach the facility, I see no more signs. Instead, I follow the car ahead of us, hoping we're headed to the same place and they know where to go. As I do, the car behind me turns to follow. Is this confirmation or the blind leading the blind?

We end up in a parking lot with nine other cars. With no hint of which building entrance to head to, we wait in our car, hoping to follow someone else. One person scurries to an uninviting alcove and disappears. Should we follow? Surely this is not the path to church. Eventually two people in the car that followed us into the parking lot exit their vehicle and head to the main doors. We follow. Unfortunately, we're not fast enough, for once we get inside, they've disappeared. I look for a sign but can't find one. I'm about to turn right when Candy tugs me left. "I think they're down there."

A couple of tables adorn the hallway, and light beams from one of the rooms. That must be the place. As we trudge down the unlit hall, a few people emerge. We move toward them.

A man greets us, and we share names. I repeat his back to him, but with a question in my voice. I heard wrong, and he corrects me. After he confirms mine, he asks if we've been there before. He doesn't think so, but he holds out the possibility we have.

"This is our first time." I smile.

He smiles back, but his glow dims. "We won't have a normal service today."

I play dumb. "Why not?"

"Our minister's gone, and one of our members will be speaking. And the minister's wife normally leads singing. She's gone too—family vacation. Someone's filling in for her too."

"So you'll have singing and a message. What do you normally do?"

"The same thing."

"So you'll still have a normal service?"

He nods at my logic, but he doesn't seem convinced.

Candy shares that we're meeting friends. He perks up at their name and quickly affirms them.

"Do you know where they usually sit?" she asks.

It seems like an unnecessary question. There are fifty chairs aligned in five neat rows and less than a dozen people present.

He thinks for a moment and bobs his head. He points to the back row. "There."

As our attempt at small talk wanes, he drifts off. With no one else who seems available for conversation, we sit down in our friends' row. The wall clock shows it's time to start, but no one seems in a hurry to do so.

I can't figure out the purpose of the space. It's far too big to be a classroom, but not large enough for anything else. The high ceiling suggests a gymnasium, but it's too small. I count the ceiling tiles and do the math: 42' by 72'. Some large matts, rolled up and against one wall, suggest this space might be for wrestling.

Since nothing's happening, Candy and I decide to visit the restrooms—in expectation of needing to sit for a ninety-minute service. There seems to be no reason to hurry, so I take my time. When I exit the restroom, I spot our friends as they arrive. We share hugs, and I attempt to interact with their kids.

We stroll to the back row as we catch up. It's been too long. Our reunion is sweet.

It seems the stated starting time is merely a guideline. Eventually the service begins, about fifteen minutes late. The man who met us when we arrived stands to greet those gathered, who now number sixteen. We and our friends make up half the group.

I think his purpose is to welcome us and give some opening remarks. From my perspective he drones on too long. His rambling comments veer political, but only vaguely so. I'm not sure of his point.

He introduces the fill-in worship leader. I don't know if this twenty-something musician is part of their community or not. With skill he moves us into our worship time. Aided with the simple sound of his acoustic guitar, he ably leads us without calling attention to himself. His focus remains rightly on God.

Some people raise their arms in praise, and I feel free to join them. Others sway gently with the melody, but my rhythmically-challenged body stands in stoic contrast. One woman edges off to the side and respectfully dances her worship. I want to watch, but don't want to intrude on her connection with the Almighty. My friend brought worship flags for her and her kids. They move behind us to praise God with the movement of their flowing banners. This must be why they sit in the back.

Though worshipful, my mind wanders at the repetition of the words and notes. With the chairs positioned in the middle of the room, open space abounds on all sides. Three banners in front proclaim "Kingdom," "Grace," and "Power." I ponder their significance. Do these words imply the Trinity? The Father's kingdom, the grace of Jesus, and the power of the Holy Spirit? Maybe. Maybe not. Am I trying to make these words fit where they don't belong?

Song lyrics project on the wall. I think our worship leader plays as he feels led, but the right words always appear at the right time. After about twenty minutes, Candy groans. I think we're still on the first song, but I'm not sure. The endless iterations weary her, whereas I just grow bored.

With a smile, I recall the cynical complaint of an old Baptist preacher about modern church music: "One word, two notes, three hours."

Eventually our numbers swell to twenty. This is less than half their normal attendance. I guess the word got out that Pastor was gone, and half the congregation did the same.

Some people may feel the presence of the Holy Spirit. I don't. For many, music acts as a conduit to God, but it seldom serves me in that way. I need quiet. Perhaps had I sat down and not tried to sing along, I would have heard from the Spirit of God.

After three or four songs, spanning forty minutes, we move into the message. An older woman stands to talk. She's nervous—both her words and her demeanor say so—but after a prayer and a few minutes she settles down and ably teaches about the righteousness of God. A former missionary, she begins with 1 Kings 8:11. "Righteousness," she says, "is to be in a condition acceptable to God." I've never heard it explained this way, but I like it.

From there she bounces around the Bible, sharing more than a half dozen related verses, teaching about each one. I jot down the verses so I can look them up later, all the while knowing I never will. I also grab some intriguing one-liners. One warrants contemplation: "Righteousness is a gift, not a goal."

After about thirty minutes she winds down. The worship leader strums his guitar as she wraps up her message. I'm not sure of the intent. She offers no altar call and gives no challenge. The service ends with a final song.

Overall, I'm disappointed. We followed their normal format, but I'm quite sure the results weren't typical. I saw little evidence of the Holy Spirit. I witnessed no baptism of the Holy Spirit, speaking in tongues, or the gifts of the spirit. There were no supernatural manifestations as their website boasted. Yes, these would have made me uncomfortable, but I know God would have revealed his truth to me anyway.

The service differed little from a low-key evangelical service, and fell far short of the charismatic experience I had hoped to encounter. I guess we should have postponed our visit until the pastor and worship leader returned.

At least we'll spend the afternoon with friends in significant spiritual community. That was the point all along and will be the highlight of our day. Church is just a prelude to the main event.

And that gives me something else to contemplate.

Takeaway for Leaders: Make sure your church website reveals what *will* happen, not what you *hope* will occur.

CHURCH #66, PART 2: A NORMAL SERVICE

Several months later we have a chance for a return visit to this same church. Again, we'll attend church with our friends and spend the afternoon together sharing our lives and faith. I look forward to both, though the time with friends outshines the chance to revisit this church. Still, the opportunity to experience a normal service with their regular pastor and new worship leader stands as a nice bonus.

Not only do we have a chance to experience one of their services with a different speaker and song leader, but they also moved since our first visit. Instead of meeting in a public-school facility, they now rent office space in a reclaimed school building in another town, about nine miles from their prior location. In most respects it will be like visiting a different church. Therefore, I view it as such.

Then I realize that it's a holiday weekend, the Sunday before Memorial Day. Many churches scale back their service and simplify their approach on holiday Sundays, especially during the summer. I wonder if we'll experience one of their typical services. Oh well. The main point of the day is a time of community with our dear friends.

Candy and I have our typical discussion about when we should leave, how long the drive will take, and when we expect to arrive. With bad weather behind us, at least we won't have road conditions to contend with.

To make our deliberations more complicated, she asks to stop at the coffee shop along the way to pick up a brew. This should add ten minutes to our trip, so we make the needed time adjustment, but when I pull into the coffee shop's parking lot I groan. There are a dozen or so cars lined up at the drive-through window.

Candy tells me not to worry. She'll go inside. That will be much faster. I want to believe her, but I don't think it will be fast enough. As it turns out, it's not. By the time we're back on the road our GPS tells us we'll arrive four minutes early and not the extra ten to fifteen minutes we'd planned on.

With the hour drive, we have a lot of time to talk, and we cover a variety of topics. This might be more time than we spent talking all week. That's something to ponder. Candy prays for the time with our friends, but I'm not sure if her prayer included church. I don't bother to ask or to tack on my own prayer for the service. The main reason for our trip is to see our friends. Going to church is a secondary goal—at least for me.

The last few minutes of our drive grow a bit harried when I realize my GPS isn't taking us to the correct location. I don't have the exact address of the church and we've forgotten its name, but Candy conducts a creative internet search to find the needed information. Ignoring the misdirection of our GPS, we drive straight to the correct place and get there four minutes early, just as our adjusted ETA predicted.

Again, an exterior sign tells us we're in the right place and indicates which entrance to use. However, once inside there are no more signs. We walk down a long corridor and eventually find an open door with the church's name on it. We exchange nervous glances and stifle our apprehension. Candy scowls at me as I graciously gesture for her to enter first. Inside is a small space, converted from a former classroom, which serves as both lobby and office.

A handful of people scurry about, each one exchanging a friendly greeting with us but nothing more. One man, however, gives me a quizzical look. We both remember each other from our prior visit, though neither can recall names. We have a brief conversation to reconnect, but, knowing that the service is about to start, Candy and I move on into a connected classroom, which serves as their worship space.

The room is square, about 30' by 30', a small fraction of the space they used to occupy. It still has fifty chairs—five rows of ten with a center aisle—but they're packed in, closer together and with little margin on the sides. Along the back wall sits the A/V equipment. On the opposite side, and on our level, is the cramped space for the worship team and minister. In the corner stand the same three banners: Grace, Kingdom, and Power. We slide into the back row, expecting to meet our friends in that general area, even though there's little room for them to wave their worship flags.

The service starts a few minutes late with a dozen or so people present. We're well into the first song when our friends arrive. We exchange hugs, and they sit in the row in front of us. Others trickle in and eventually our numbers swell to about thirty. I could count, but I'm tired of counting the number of church attendees and merely make an educated estimate. The crowd is mostly female, skewing older, as are all the couples. I see no men by themselves.

The worship leader is the same one we had last time, which I later learn was his first time leading worship at this church. Again, he plays guitar as he leads. An idle keyboard sits next to him, and he serves as our only musician and singer. He has an easy, smooth style, without being slickly polished. It's hard to tell how much he rehearsed and how much happens as he feels led by the Holy Spirit.

The singing goes on longer than I would like, and I know Candy must be fidgeting on the inside. I'm not sure how many songs we sing because they're interwoven with each other, and we keep looping back to repeat choruses. She later tells me there were only four songs, which filled up most of an hour. Through it all, I try to worship God, but we don't really connect. I guess I should've made a better effort at praying for this service beforehand.

My friend turns around and whispers that they have open communion, and we can go up anytime we want—if we wish to—during the singing. I nod, even though I've already decided not to. I share this information with Candy, and she agrees. I may have missed it, but I only see four or five people go forward for communion. Curious.

About half an hour into the music set, several people ease their way forward and surround a young man sitting alone in the front row, who I guess is the pastor. They place their hands on him and their lips move in quiet prayer. Then they sit down. I assume the message is about to begin, but it doesn't. We have more singing to do.

By the time he finally moves to the front, we've been

singing for over an hour. He gives several announcements. Then he shares some news. The worship leader guiding us in song this service is no longer their backup, fill-in musician. Effective today he's their new worship pastor. The minister explains what the worship pastor's role will entail and confirms they didn't force out the prior worship leaders. They'll still help lead worship when their busy schedules allow. This meets everyone's approval. Then we have the offering.

Before the sermon the pastor has a time of prayer, which includes prophecies, words of encouragement, and prayers for healing as the Holy Spirit directs him. He feels led to pray for the needs of a woman in the congregation and invites other women to gather around her in support, if they wish. This subtle distinction keeps men at a distance, a wise action to foster a safe environment.

Then he moves into his sermon, starting with a lengthy review of last week's message based on Luke 5:17–26. It's hard to know where the review ends and today's sermon begins, especially since he says he interjected new material into last week's review. By my reckoning, he spent more time on the review than on today's lesson.

Today's starting text is Mark 5:24–34. His style is fluid as he jumps from one passage to the next. After a while I stop noting the Scripture references, but I do write down two thought-provoking one-liners.

First, "Don't preach against other religions. Preach Jesus and the Gospel." Over the years, I've heard too many preachers who didn't follow this advice. They were so quick to condemn the practices and ideas of others that they forgot about the good news of Jesus. This might be a contributing factor as to why the public has such a negative view of Christians: we rant about what we're against and don't celebrate what we're for.

In the other one he states, "The Law was given to the Jews, not the Gentiles." This one merits serious contemplation. It could change how I understand and apply the Old Testament.

He says he spends most of his week in prayer and Bible study, admitting he prefers that over meeting with people and attending to congregational needs. Our friends later confirmed his deep dedication to his relationship with God and God's Word.

Indeed, his teaching flows as one who spends much time with God and immerses himself in the Bible. When he shares a verse, I never see him glancing at his notes first. The text and the reference gush forth as regular speech. I wonder how many of his words are something he planned to say and how many come to him from the Holy Spirit just before they leave his mouth. I suspect the latter.

Unfortunately, I'm tired and stifle yawns throughout the sermon. It's not that I'm bored. I just didn't sleep well last night. Had I been more alert, I would have gotten much more out of his message.

At 12:30, two hours after the service began, he stops preaching. He's not at a stopping point that I can tell, and he has no conclusion or call to action. He merely says he'll pick up next week. As he's doing this, the worship leader slides up to the front. He picks up his guitar and begins playing softly. We sing a song, and the pastor prays. As he wraps up his prayer, he turns his attention to Candy. He perceives she has a physical need for healing or restoration, a need she may not even know exists. He prays for her as the Holy Spirit leads him.

Then he wraps up the service, and we leave. Anticipated time with friends around a delicious meal beckons us.

It's several hours before Candy and I can discuss our experience at this church. In all our many church visits, few, if any, have been this spirit-led. Though, unlike our other Pentecostal and charismatic experiences, I feel the Holy Spirit powerfully directed our time together through both the teaching pastor and the worship leader.

As for Candy, she's upset over the prophetic words of healing the pastor directed to her. She doesn't know of any physical issue. I point out that this was a draining week for her, emotionally and mentally. I suggest he was just a bit off when he said she had a physical need. She doesn't buy this.

Then I share the concept of performance anxiety. It could be he so wanted to hear a word from God to give to the visitors that he overstretched, that he perceived something that wasn't there. I get this. Sometimes people who follow the Holy Spirit's leading don't bat 1,000. Sometimes they hit a home run, sometimes they get a single, and other times they strike out. I'm okay with this, but it's hard for Candy to accept.

Regardless, going to church with our friends was a great experience. It showed us a way to worship God and function in community that I don't see at many churches.

Takeaway for Everyone: Don't rant about what you're against. Celebrate what you're for.

CHURCH #67: SATELLITE CHURCH

I'm not sure why it works out this way, but it's another holiday weekend, and we're off to visit another church. This one is three-quarters of a mile from our home. We could walk to it, and consider doing so, but we talk ourselves out of it. Part of the issue is that I don't know how long it will take to walk there. I think ten minutes will do it, but what if it's twenty? Instead we opt to drive.

We're meeting family there, visiting this church together, the first time for all of us. I've been curious about this church since they launched two years ago. This is the first time Candy expressed a willingness to go.

This isn't a new church, not really. It's a satellite location of an established church. Unlike many satellite churches, however, this one offers its music and message live. There's no remote feed from the main location.

Their model is straightforward. The parent church, one of the larger ones in the area, has been launching satellite sites for several years. I believe this marks their fifth. Each location has a teaching pastor and its own worship team, with centralized governance and financial control.

I've heard of this arrangement before and know of two churches that attempted it. In both cases, things didn't work out as planned. Early in the process the launch team at both sites decided they didn't want to be a satellite location. Instead they wanted independence and to form their own congregation. What started as a satellite location turned into a church plant. This church has avoided this problem and seems to have fine-tuned the art of opening satellite locations.

When they launched this site, they coupled it with a smart direct-mail campaign to people in the surrounding area. That's how we learned about them, and that's why I longed to visit. Today we will.

They meet at the local middle school, an arrangement I find most attractive. Instead of investing money in a building that's only fully used a few hours each week and is only a fraction occupied during business hours, they free up money to invest in outreach and ministry. Yes, they do have the expense of rent, but that's much less than what it would cost to own and maintain a building. In addition, if they outgrow this facility, they can simply rent a different one. However, if you outgrow a building you own, you have limited options. So in addition to the cost factor, I appreciate this arrangement for its flexibility.

As we approach the entrance to the middle school, the church's trailer sits alongside the driveway, smartly doubling as a sign for the church and signaling the proper entrance. Renting space from a school means they need to set up and tear down each Sunday. The large trailer doubles as a transportation unit on Sunday and storage space throughout the week for their needed equipment and supplies.

We pull in and drive past the trailer. There are two lots, with cars parked in both. I wonder which one to head to, accompanied by the question of which building entrance to use. My deliberation is short-lived. A large vertical welcome banner waves by both entrances off both parking lots. Apparently each entrance works equally well. I pull into the first lot and park our car. We head to the closest entrance, staffed with two smiling greeters.

We walk up and engage in easy small talk. I feel free to linger because there are no people behind us waiting to get in. It's nice not to feel rushed, even though we didn't leave home as early as I wanted. The drive took less than two minutes, and we arrived twelve minutes early. Entering, we walk down the short hallway. There's no question about where to go. Another portable sign tells us to turn right for the church service, though the nursery and some children's programs are to the left. We veer right and find ourselves in a large open space, with people mingling about.

As we move forward, two men interrupt their conversation to talk to us, something I seldom witness at the churches we visit. They share their names, and we give ours, making a connection with them as we do. They're both involved in the worship team, but one has the summer off. The other will play today. He's on drums. After a few minutes, he excuses himself to join the rest of the worship team. We talk with the other man a little longer. He's not outgoing, but he's friendly and easy enough to talk to.

We thank him for his attention and move into the worship space, a typical middle school gymnasium. It's large enough for two basketball courts running left to right, or one running the other direction, with retractable bleachers to provide a nice-sized viewing area. Thankfully, we will not be sitting in the bleachers.

In the middle of the gymnasium are folding chairs set in three sections, with one hundred chairs per section. We sit down as we wait for the rest of our family to arrive and for the service to begin, wondering which will happen first. As it turns out, both occur at the same time.

The overhead lights are off. What light we do have comes from indirect lighting. The subdued ambiance in the room makes it hard to read the literature they gave us when we walked in.

The space begins to fill. All age groups show up, but the demographics skew younger, with many families present. It's likely that most of the tweens and younger teenagers here today also attend this school during the week, and their younger siblings will go here in a few years. As we wait for the service to start, the interlude is agreeable. Soft music plays in the background. People talk with friends before the service begins. The atmosphere strikes a pleasing middle ground between churches whose members sit in stoic silence for their service to start and those where an excess of activity overwhelms.

A worship team of five gathers up front. In addition to our new friend, the drummer, there are two on guitars, one on keys, and one backup vocalist. They have no one for bass. The keyboardist doubles as the worship leader. All are male. I wonder if that's intentional or how things worked out today. Also, four-fifths of their ensemble fit within the millennial generation, with one lone baby boomer.

They launch into their first song, which, thankfully, is familiar to me. The Bible tells us to sing a new song to God

(Psalm 96:1), but encountering only unfamiliar tunes and hard-to-sing lyrics is off-putting when visiting churches. The worship team's leading in song is quite effective, though they lack an accomplished edge to separate them from the typical worship team at a midsize church. Since it's a holiday weekend, we may not have their A-team leading us. Regardless, their sincerity in what they do is evident. Their hearts seem in the right place.

After the first song, the teaching pastor welcomes us. He's been on a sabbatical this summer, and this is his first Sunday back. He's glad to return and gives some announcements. One is something they call "Breaking Bread." It's a chance to get to know others in the church. The idea is simple: three individuals or families agree to get together three times in the next three months around a shared meal, dessert, or coffee. Interested families sign up, and the church assigns the groups. This helps people get to know others and form connections. It's a short-term commitment with a long-term benefit.

Then the pastor moves us into the greeting time. I interact with four people, two young boys who play along with the ritual and two adults. The boys offer wide smiles and immature handshakes. I appreciate their effort. One adult keeps her interaction with me to a minimum, while the other one takes time to share her name and ask mine.

And yet after these four, no one else makes any effort to offer a greeting. I fidget a bit, longing for this time to end. Fortunately, I don't need to wait long. As church greetings go, this one is neither memorable nor haunting. I survived it.

Our space is now over half full. We launch into more singing, a five-song set. I don't know any of the songs, but I'm able to pick up the chorus on most of them and the

More Than 52 Churches

verses on a few others. Next is the offering. I wasn't listening, but I don't believe there was any mention that visitors need not participate. Not that I would have felt any obligation, but it's a nice gesture, especially given that a common complaint against churches is, "They're only after your money."

There's an information card to fill out and drop in the offering baskets as they pass by, but Candy's still working on it when the offering gets to us. We'll turn the card in after the service. The offering wraps up, and they slide smoothly into one more song before the sermon begins. They've added more chairs in the back, which are now mostly occupied. I suspect the sanctuary attendance is now pushing three hundred. In addition, I guess a hundred or more kids and their leaders are off doing their own activities.

After his break from preaching, the teaching pastor is more than ready to deliver our message. It looks like it's week three of a three-part series. He doesn't recap weeks one and two, but I surmise the key points from the series title: "Belong, Believe, Become." I've heard these three words strung together at other churches, so I have a good idea of what the prior two sermons covered. Today is about *becoming*. Yet if there's a title for today's message, I missed it.

Our scripture text is from Matthew 16:13–18. He says this is one of his favorite chapters in the Bible and is glad to speak on it. The passage is about Jesus and his disciples traveling to Caesarea Philippi, a corrupt place far different than the less appalling environments he and his disciples typically frequent.

What might the disciples have thought as they traveled to this place, a destination that good Jewish boys avoid? When they arrive, Jesus asks them, "Who do people say I am?" After various answers, Peter says, "You are the Messiah, the Son of the Living God."

That's when Jesus says to Peter, which means *rock*, "On this rock I will build my church." I've heard sermons on this passage. People debate the meaning of this last phrase. Some say Peter is the rock on which God will build his church. Others assert that Peter's confession, that Jesus is the Messiah, is the foundational statement which will support the church. A third understanding looks at the setting—which ties in with the image of a rock— and the depraved behavior of the people in this area. This may be the rock on which Jesus will build his church. Why else would Jesus take them twenty miles to ask them a question he could have asked at any other time?

The point I derive from this is to take the good news of Jesus to the people who most need it. As I contemplate the implication of this, I jot down a soundbite from the minister. He says, "Know your community." This makes sense. If we're going to reach our neighbors, we should understand them better.

He talks about two kinds of community. One is the church's internal community, and the other is the community around us. He gives us a simple three-point process to engage people: Step one is to talk to them. Step two is to ask them a question. Finally, step three is to invite them for a meal, an outing, or a service opportunity. Most people, both those within and outside the church, are open to an invitation to do something.

He concludes with an encouragement to build church where we are.

The service ends, and two things happen at once. One is that most people pick up their chair, collapse it, and stow it on a nearby rack. The other is that people come up to us to talk. Some recognize Candy from her involvement in the community, and others are strangers, extending gracious welcomes. We enjoy these conversations, which are friendly and engaging.

After doing my part to pick up our family's chairs, we move back into the lobby. There we turn in our visitor cards, and they offer us a gift. I suspect it will be a coffee mug or travel cup, and I also know Candy will pass. We already have a cabinet stuffed full of them. She declines the offer with grace, and we enjoy an extended time of conversation at the visitor center, with a most engaging woman.

She tells us about their church, and we ask her questions. Many thoughts bombard my mind, but the one question I do ask is how next Sunday's service will compare to this holiday weekend experience. With a knowing nod, the woman affirms the service will be the same format. The only difference will be the number of people present.

I wonder how many more people but don't ask. We could return next week to find out. In two weeks, they'll have an after-church event for people who want to learn more about their gathering. It may be worth coming back for that too. This church has much to offer.

I long to go to church in my community and attend with my neighbors. This church meets the first criteria, but I don't spot any neighbors. Perhaps if we come back on a regular Sunday, I might see some of them here. It's a hopeful thought.

Takeaway for Everyone: How you engage with first-time visitors determines how likely they are to return.

CHURCH #68: URBAN ON A MISSION

Candy and I live in a homogenous area of mostly white, middle class families residing in a suburban setting, sitting on the edge of rural. Our community has minimal diversity and our area churches, even less. Most of my life I've lived in settings with people like me. Our current home is like our others. The neighborhood, both comfortable and stable, stands as a safe place sheltered from the world around it.

We chose this general location to be near family and this setting for its amenities and ambiance. We didn't intentionally set out to segregate ourselves. It just happened. However, we weren't deliberate about seeking a more diverse environment, either. Even though we couldn't have achieved this goal along with our other objectives, it still pains me. What hurts me more is to know that if we visit an area church, it will be a mostly white experience.

When a friend mentions an urban church in a nearby

city, I'm excited. I can't experience much diversity where I live without moving, but I can experience it through my church selection. Based on this church's location and its desire to serve the inner city, I anticipate meeting people of other races and expect a service style relevant to its neighborhood.

It takes some effort, but I eventually find their website. They're an evangelical community of Christians committed to "intentional discipleship." I have no idea why they put *intentional discipleship* in quotes, but it calls attention to the phrase, though in a curious way. The phrase appears multiple times on their home page. It must be important.

I also know to expect "verse-by-verse Bible teaching." Next I learn they're "a multi-racial and multi-socioeconomic relational community," a "true urban church," where "the homeless worship side-by-side and support one another in Christ."

Their website also talks about community outreach, including serving at the community kitchen, inner city street events, and downtown student fellowship—the campus of a Christian college is only a couple of blocks away. Surely their urban setting allows for these things to happen. I'm excited for what we'll encounter when we visit.

I tell Candy it's a thirty-minute drive and she accepts this, even though online resources put it at twenty-four. We add a ten-minute buffer and plan to leave forty minutes early, but I doubt we will. I wonder about parking. In truth, I *worry* about parking. I know there's limited street parking in the area, and I have no clue about parking lots in the vicinity. The church's website doesn't help, giving only a street number.

As we head out, thirty minutes early, we pray for God's blessing during our time at this church, that we will be an encouragement to those we meet, and God will show us what he wants us to learn. Silently, I add my request that we'll find a place to park, one that is both close and safe.

After my prayer, I breathe a bit easier and my shoulders relax—just a little. Whatever happens will happen, and worrying about it won't change a thing. We once attended an urban church. Ironically, back then it was Candy who had concerns about safety when walking from our parked car to the church and then back again.

This church meets in an old warehouse, which they just started using. I like the idea of churches meeting in reclaimed spaces, as opposed to going to the expense of constructing a huge church building that they'll only use a few hours a week. For them to meet in a downtown area, using existing space is their only option.

I navigate the one-way streets, needing to overshoot our destination and approach it from the other side. As we get closer, my pulse quickens with apprehension about the parking situation and for the unknown that awaits us inside. With one block to go, I wipe my sweaty hands on my jeans. My heart pounds. I strive to keep my fears to myself.

Ahead, I spot a sign for the church on the sidewalk, with a few people mingling around the entrance. To my left is a city parking lot. I thank God and pull in. There are empty spots awaiting us and, as a bonus, we don't need to pay because it's the weekend. I worried for nothing, but then, most of the things we worry about never happen anyway. Still, I give credit to Papa for answered prayer and a place to park.

More Than 52 Churches

The surrounding area is nice. It's well-kept and clean. We feel safe. As we walk from the parking lot to the building, another family approaches from the opposite direction and others walk from across the street. Both groups wear smiles and carry crockpots. I groan.

"Looks like there's a potluck," I whisper to Candy. A time around a shared meal is a great way to connect with others and build community, but I regret coming empty-handed. Once more on our adventure of visiting churches, we'll be freeloaders. They'll surely welcome us generously and invite us to stay, insisting there will be plenty of food. Nonetheless, I'll feel a tad guilty for receiving what they'll share, offering nothing in return.

I also know that instead of a two-hour church meeting, we'll have a three-hour church community experience. Since we have no other plans for this afternoon, this isn't a problem, but I do need to mentally adjust my thinking for how long we will be here. I don't do well with handling the unexpected, but God graciously enables me to accept this twist as an adventure.

Two people welcome us before we enter the building and more folks greet us inside. They share two important pieces of information. The first is the location of the sanctuary and the other is directions to the restrooms, which are on another floor and not close by. Good to know.

The worship space is a large banquet hall, reclaimed from what was once a warehouse. Along one side of the rectangular space sits a slightly-raised stage, the focal point of the service, with musical instruments and gear for the worship team. In front of it is a communion table, an altar of sorts. On the opposite wall, a row of tables lines the other side, already filling with the food we'll enjoy in a couple of hours. In the space between stand fifteen round tables, with seven chairs each. That calculates to 105 seats.

So that we won't need to contort our necks or pivot our chairs to participate in the service, I look for a table that has open seats facing the front. Few people are sitting, but others have claimed most of the forward-facing chairs, marked with Bibles, purses, and coffee mugs.

At the far end of the room, I spot one open table and scoot toward it, grabbing the two forward-facing spots. As we settle down, another couple joins us, and we spend time getting to know each other. They're friendly, and we make a quick connection. Then the wife of this couple excuses herself to join the worship team as it assembles in the front.

Six people lead us in singing. The lead vocalist also plays keyboard. Our new friend plays violin. Joining them are a bass guitar player and a drummer, along with two backup vocalists. For the next forty-five minutes we sing, mostly modern choruses and one updated hymn.

We stand as we sing. Some of the seventy or so people present raise their hands in praise as they sing to God, while a few gently move their bodies in a subtle form of physical worship. With plenty of space, I can freely raise my arms without bumping into people—a common occurrence given the tight seating at most churches.

The crowd is mostly older, fifty plus if I'm being generous, but over sixty is more likely. There are few kids, one set with their grandparents and another set who we later find out are visiting. The crowd is white and not the amalgamation of races I had anticipated.

I don't spot anyone who looks—or smells—homeless.

Having been part of an urban church for eight years, one which attracted a large contingency of homeless, I'm used to being around them. Could the homeless in this area be a more upscale version than what I know? Ones who enjoy regular access to showers and washing machines, who have clothes that match. Aside from the urban setting, this doesn't look much like an urban church. We don't ask, and no one explains the lack of diversity that their website promised.

We have a reading from Psalm 148, followed by a meditation. Next is the offertory prayer and the offering. After this we move into a time of prayer. They share specific concerns—mostly health and work related—for the people present. Some people gather around those near them who need prayer and pray for them. Next is a ministry update and more prayer.

People in the congregation take an active part in all of this. At this point, we've only heard from the teaching pastor two brief times. This is more how a church gathering should function, with people ministering to one another.

Now at an hour into the service, we take a fifteen-minute break. This allows us time to meet more people. We don't need to mingle to do this. They come up to us. Most everyone asks where we live and are amazed at how far we traveled to visit them. When I ask them the same question, I'm surprised to learn that not one of them lives in the downtown area. Everyone we talked to drove from suburbia or the country to reach this urban setting. Curious.

During this interlude, a prayer team is available to pray for people. A line never forms, but they keep busy as people approach them for prayer.

The sermon is "Let the Church be the Church" and the

text is Philippians 1:1–2. The interior of the bulletin offers a two-page spread, packed with sermon notes, complete with over fifty blanks for us to fill in. I skip this, knowing I'll become so fixated on filling in every blank that I'll miss the actual message. Candy, however, is up for the challenge and fills in most of them.

For forty-five minutes, the pastor tells us about elders and deacons, about God's grace and peace. In doing so, he pulls in much related teaching from other passages in the Bible, adding much to the text. This isn't the verse-by-verse Bible teaching that the website promised, but a springboard text that serves as a preface for expanded instruction.

His informed teaching is interesting, but I don't grasp a central point or purpose in what he shares. As he concludes, his message takes an evangelical turn, reminding us to pray for one person to lead to Jesus.

We then quickly move into the potluck, with a bounty of food—much of it left over from a wedding reception the day before. Many people invite us to stay, almost relieved when we say "yes."

With so many who reach out to us, we're among the last to get in line to select our food. Even lining up late, there's still plenty to eat, at least twice the amount needed. In true potluck style, I take a little bit of most everything and end up with a plate heaped full of more than I should eat. It tastes so good. Good food, good fellowship, and good times. This is more of what church should be.

We interact with more people. All are friendly and engaging. Through it all, we suffer through no awkward moments that too often happen at churches where people don't welcome well or don't welcome at all. This, however, is an engaging group. They're intentional about their faith and their life.

I'm glad we experienced community with them. God, bless them and their work for your kingdom.

Takeaway for Everyone: Are visitors glad to experience community with you or glad to leave as soon as they can?

OTHER CONSIDERATIONS

I have three more churches on my spreadsheet to visit. In addition, I have four more on my mental list. I consider adding these other four churches to my spreadsheet, but for some reason I don't. I think we should first go to the remaining three churches before adding four more. Unfortunately, we're doing a bad job at moving forward and going to those first three. That means the next four will have to wait even longer.

At the same time, I wonder if it's time to wrap up this project. This isn't because I feel there's nothing left to explore, but because I think I've given this venture all I have left to give. Besides, Candy has been supportive of this journey, and I don't want to push past her willingness to cheerfully be part of it.

CHURCH #69: SUFFERING FROM A BAD RAP

First on our list is a church from a small conservative denomination. Their denomination website says they have thirty-three churches in North America, eleven of which are within driving distance from our house. The closest one is five miles away. In contrast, they have five more international locations.

I've never met anyone who currently goes to one of this denomination's churches. In the past few years, however, I've met several people who *used* to go there. Their stories are similar and worrisome. They left this church bruised and bloodied, rejected by the people they used to worship with. Sometimes they're spurned by their family and friends who continue to go to these churches. Although there are two sides to every story, their accounts of what happened breaks my heart. That's because their perspective of what caused their separation seems to be over trivial matters.

Every church has people who think poorly of it. As long as we're frail humans with a nature to sin, this will occur.

Sometimes the reasons for these low opinions are justified and other times they're self-inflicted. However, to only meet people who harbor hurts from this denomination is troublesome.

I want to visit one of these churches to learn more about them. But I already know too much and couldn't go with an open mind. I would look for the negative, hunting for areas to criticize so I can justify the depths of my friends' pain. Surely, I would find the validation I seek. I fear I wouldn't have eyes to see the good in their practices, truly worship God with them, or celebrate meaningful community while I was there.

Until I can properly adjust my perspective, I need to hold off visiting them. Unfortunately, after a couple of years of trying, I'm no closer to being successful. For this reason, their church keeps moving down my list as we visit other congregations.

Takeaway for Everyone: What is your church's reputation? What can you do about it?

CHURCH #70: UNPLANNED AND SPONTANEOUS

A few years ago, I stumbled upon a group of Young Quakers online. Their faith, their passion for community, and their desire to make a difference in their world drew me in. They even invited me to their annual gathering, halfway across the country. Though I had never met one of them in person, for a time I even considered going. That's how desperate I was to be part of a vibrant faith community—even for a weekend. They were all about half my age, which may explain their zest and their appeal to me. After serious consideration, however, I opted not to go.

Being ever practical, I looked for a gathering closer to home. Some of their group met on the other side of the state, but that was still too far away. Casting a wider net for Quakers in general, I found a gathering some forty minutes from my house. They don't meet every week, but instead get together the first, third, and fifth Sundays of each month.

According to their website, their meetings are unplanned

and spontaneous. They use different wording, but my take is they spend a lot of time listening to the Holy Spirit, responding as appropriate. Sometimes this means sharing insights and other times it entails keeping it to themselves. With no minister, everyone can participate in an egalitarian manner.

This is quite different from my normal Sunday practices, yet I have often experienced this, albeit without my bride, in other settings. There we would quiet ourselves and wait for the Holy Spirit to speak to us. If his words were for the group, we would share them. Otherwise, we would keep his insight to ourselves. I wrote what I heard in my journal.

I know Candy would go to this church without complaint, but I also worry that their format would make her uncomfortable. I never resolved this dilemma, so the Quakers also kept moving down the list as we visited other churches.

Of note: In my online research about Quakers, I gather there is a wide range of Quaker practices. On one side are those gatherings that focus on the leading of the Holy Spirit, as this church seems to follow. In contrast, other Quaker meetings are quite different.

Takeaway for Leaders: Does your church website tell visitors what they can expect when they visit? Is it accurate?

CHURCH #71: A MESSIANIC JEWISH CONGREGATION

Before *52 Churches*, we visited a Messianic Jewish church: Jews who believe in Jesus as their Jewish savior, mixing Jewish tradition with Christian faith.

They met on Saturday nights. The service involved a time of worship and a time of teaching. They concluded with a shared meal. Most of the service was in English, but a few parts of worship were in Hebrew. I mumbled the words the best I could, but I had no idea if my fellow worshipers pronounced their Hebrew words correctly or not.

Their hymnals were in both Hebrew and English. As I recall, page one was at the back. For their meal, shared potluck style, they provided food with a Jewish flair. I don't know how authentic or Americanized these dishes were, but they were tasty.

The friendly people there embraced us. They welcomed us. We felt like family from the beginning. Worshiping God in an unfamiliar way brought a freshness, an authenticity to our efforts. Their unfamiliar traditions occasionally confused me, but I also felt strangely invigorated by what we did.

They didn't have their own building, but they did have their own worship space. It was in the basement of a Protestant church. This was ideal, since neither group used the facility at the same time.

There were two interesting things about this congregation. First, everyone there was Gentile. That is, they weren't Jewish. It seems strange to me that a Messianic Jewish church wouldn't have some Jewish people attending it. When I asked about this, someone explained that sometimes a Jewish family did drive from another city to meet with them, but this didn't occur every week.

The other interesting thing is most of the people present at this Saturday evening Messianic Jewish gathering also attend a Protestant service on Sunday morning. This perplexed me. However, this is exactly what Candy and I did.

That was many years ago, but the experience stayed with me, and I want to encounter it again. When we embarked upon our *52 Churches* journey, I desired to include this church and make a repeat visit. Unfortunately, they no longer met at the same place. Instead their location rotated between the homes of their regular attendees. Revisiting them wasn't going to work for *52 Churches*. And though I would've liked to have returned later, we never got around to it.

There's another Messianic Jewish congregation near where we live. It's a thirty-five-minute drive, not close but not insurmountable either. I want to visit them and compare their practices with my recollection of the first Messianic Jewish congregation.

I want to go. We could go. But we don't.

I guess I'm tired of visiting churches.

Takeaway for Leaders: What can you do to encourage people who think about visiting your church but never get around to it?

CHURCH #72: RESPECTED AND ESTEEMED

In addition to these three remaining churches on my spreadsheet is my mental list of four more.

The first of these churches is the Salvation Army. Most people know the Salvation Army for their red donation kettles at Christmastime. Beyond that, they focus on the needs of the homeless and provide disaster relief and humanitarian aid throughout the year. But they're also a church. Few people know this. I'd like to experience one of their services.

The Salvation Army is an organization I think highly of. I suspect everyone does. Though I've heard people complain about various streams of Christianity and even more so Protestant denominations and specific churches, I've yet to hear any negativity about the Salvation Army. The closest thing I've heard to a complaint is people who wish they wouldn't ring their bells quite so much at their donation kettles during Christmas. But that's hardly a criticism of their organization.

Instead, people respect the Salvation Army for the positive impact they make in their community and around the world. Their practical service to those in need earns the esteem of both the faithful and the faithless. Helping one person at a time, they make a difference in our world, serving as the hands and feet of Jesus.

Someday I'll visit this church. Their closest location is thirty minutes away, but for now I'll put going there on hold.

Takeaway for Everyone: What do both Christians and non-Christians think of your church? What are you doing to make a difference in your community and around the world?

CHURCH #73: A DEBATABLE DESTINATION

Next on my mental list of churches to visit sits a contentious consideration. I refer to Mormon, The Church of Jesus Christ of Latter-day Saints (LDS for short). I read that most Mormons consider themselves Christians, whereas most non-Mormon Christians don't, viewing them as a sect or even a cult. Vitriol emerges.

I suspect this non-Christian label, however, comes mostly from a lack of good information. The Mormons Candy and I know exemplify Christian talk, behavior, and beliefs—more so than a lot of Christians we know.

Most people I've talked with about the subject hold strong views on the topic. Yet their opinions are seldom based on firsthand experience. Instead, they form their assessment using secondhand information and citing the views of others, which may spring from questionable motives.

Mormons hold to some beliefs that non-Mormons have difficulty accepting or comprehending. Yet, I suspect, the same holds true for every Christian church in existence. At our various churches we all do things that seem normal to us as insiders and questionable to those on the outside looking in.

The closest LDS church is a fifteen-minute drive away, making it the most accessible of any of these final four churches under consideration. Still, I remain undecided if we should visit or not. As such, this remains an academic consideration and nothing more.

Takeaway for Everyone: What is your view of churches that hold beliefs and practices quite different from yours? What can you do to promote Christian unity among these disparate views?

CHURCH #74: AN INTRIGUING MYSTERY

Another church is Anglican Catholic. They're also on my mental list of churches to visit. I expect their service to be much like Roman Catholic, but I'm not sure. To compare them with Roman Catholicism and other high churches might offer good insight. I'm sure I can learn much and gather even more to contemplate about our common faith and our varied worship practices.

Unlike other streams of Christianity and other Protestant denominations, I've never met anyone who was Anglican Catholic—at least not that I'm aware of. Since I know nothing about them and don't even have secondhand information to base an assessment on, they emerge for me with a mystical aura. I doubt that's an accurate perception, but based on my lack of knowledge, it's all I have. Are they more like Catholicism or Protestantism? Does this question even matter?

To clarify my thinking, remove misconceptions, and inform a more accurate understanding will require an in-person visit. There's an Anglican Catholic church within a half hour drive of our home. But until we can visit, I'll have to consider them from a distance as an intriguing mystery to explore.

Takeaway for Everyone: What can you do to help people better understand your church's worship and practices?

CHURCH #75: FATIGUE AND FEAR SET IN

My final consideration is Greek Orthodox. They appear fourth on my mental list of churches to visit. Like Anglican Catholic, I've never talked to anyone who was Greek Orthodox or Eastern Orthodox. Historically, I understand they split from the Roman Catholic Church about a thousand years ago.

What little I know—accurate or not—comes from what I've seen in movies and television. This is hardly an ideal source of information of what it means to be Greek Orthodox and how their worship of God unfolds. Visiting them could be another high church experience, which I could contrast to Roman Catholic and Anglican Catholic.

A Greek Orthodox church is about thirty minutes away. Yet inertia keeps me from visiting. In truth, I suspect an element of fear also conspires to keep me away, not that I haven't had to deal with my share of fear in visiting many of the other churches. But now, a certain degree of church-visiting fatigue contrives to make me unsure and keep me away.

This isn't their issue, it's mine. Given this, I wonder how many other people have similar concerns that keep them home on Sunday and thwart them from visiting churches, one of which could turn out to be a great faith community for them to plug into.

Takeaway for Members: Might people say they've never talked to anyone who was part of your church or faith community? What can you do to change that, if even for only one person?

OUR HOME CHURCH

For *52 Churches*, we took a year off and visited a different Christian church every Sunday. When the year wrapped up, we returned to our home church.

This time it's different. Throughout *More Than 52 Churches*, we interspersed our church visits with regular attendance at our home church. This provided a balance, a stability to keep us anchored in church community, as we visited others.

Attending our home church required a fifteen-minute trip to get there, going past many other options that were more accessible and more inviting.

For much of my life, I couldn't figure out why we drove past other churches to go to our church of choice. Yet we never went to the closest one. Since each Christian church worships the same God, follows the same Savior, and reads the same Bible, it shouldn't really matter which one we go to. Yes, this is theoretical. I do understand why most people don't go to the closest church.

More Than 52 Churches

For years, I've longed to go to church in my community, worshiping and serving with my neighbors and family.

Now we do.

It's Church #67, the "Satellite Church."

After our initial visit, we returned the following week, and came back the week after that, staying for their after-church meeting to learn more about their community. Soon going there turned into a habit, and we got involved. This may explain in part why the allure of visiting other churches grew dim.

This church is within walking distance of our house, three-quarters of a mile away. (For full disclosure, this is the second-closest church. There's one a tad nearer. We visited it, but one of us didn't care for it.)

We now know that several of our neighbors attend our church, as well as two of our children and grandchildren. Weather permitting, I walk to church each Sunday. Candy drives. This way we can leave church together and head for lunch with family.

It's all good.

It's our new church home.

Takeaway for Leaders: How many of your church's attendees are from your neighborhood, and how many come from other communities? What can you do to attract more locals?

HOW TO BE AN ENGAGING CHURCH

The experiences I share in this book are just that: my experiences. Other people will have different observations when visiting a church. I am an introvert, as is a slight majority of the population, but my reactions are not unique to or representative of introverts. Indeed, everyone, both introvert and extrovert, will share my perspective to varying degrees—some more profoundly and others less so. Regardless, know that I have never talked with anyone who claimed they could visit a new church without some degree of anxiety.

Also know that I had a most supportive wife accompanying me each week (except for the week she was out of town and I went solo: Church #61, "The Wrong Time to Visit"). With her at my side, I stood much braver than I would have on my own. Even so, I had to fight the urge to make a U-turn in the parking lot at Church #54 ("Emergent Maybe") and pray earnestly to stave off a bit of a panic attack while walking into Church #58 ("Not So Friendly").

Visiting a church with a non-supportive spouse would be even harder, as well as showing up by yourself. Given all this, it's easy to see why someone with even the best intentions of visiting a church will decide not to. Instead, they'll maintain their Sunday morning status quo—whether staying home or attending the church they know, even if it's the wrong one. Sticking with what we're used to is so much easier than confronting our fears and going someplace unknown.

That's why it's so critical for a church to do everything possible to make it less scary for a visitor to show up. Being a welcoming church is a great start, but it's not enough. Churches need to go beyond welcoming visitors. They need to engage with them. You must be a disarming church, likeable, even irresistible.

There are many factors that make a church engaging. Three recurring themes emerged from our visits to other churches. These stand out as essential skills to master.

Make it Easy for Visitors

Most people today go online to find information. This includes someone thinking about visiting your church. Therefore, having an attractive, up-to-date, and visitor-friendly website is key.

A few churches try to skip this step by establishing their online home base on various social media sites. This, however, is shortsighted. Social media platforms can change their rules of engagement at any time, restrict who sees your information, and even summarily shut you down without notice. Yes, a church can still have social media pages, but these should direct visitors to the church website, which the church owns and controls.

As mentioned, the website must be attractive. It should look current and be easy to navigate. It must follow best practices. This means your website needs a makeover every couple of years, or else it will look dated, which will cause visitors to dismiss your church as out of touch.

Next, your website needs current information. Remove obsolete content and add new info as soon as changes occur. Nothing will cause website visitors to bounce from your site faster—and dismiss your church quicker—than when it includes information that's no longer relevant.

A third key is accuracy. Some church websites are as misleading as dating profiles. (Not that I have any firsthand experience with dating websites, but I've heard that embellished claims abound). Some church websites paint a picture of what the church once was but no longer is, while other sites present an image of what they want to become. Both are lies and seriously mislead visitors, which results in disappointment. This causes first-time church visitors to become one-time visitors.

As far as the specific information a website should have, clear and easy to find service times are critical. Don't make people search for this or wonder if what they find is accurate.

Just as important is your street address. Unless your location is well known and highly visible, assume visitors will use their GPS to get there. Make it easy for them to do so.

Next, people will wonder what they should wear to feel comfortable at your church. And even if you don't care what they wear, they will. They'll want to fit in, so let them know how most people dress. Is your church come-as-you-are, business casual, or Sunday best? Somewhere in between?

If you have multiple services, note the times. Highlight any differences, such as in format, music content, and sermon style. Also note any other Sunday programming you may offer. Do you have Sunday school? Is it concurrent to the service or at a different time? Do you have something separate for teens? What about college students or young singles? These are two demographics that many churches overlook.

Let newcomers know what to expect. Beyond explaining a typical service, tell them what they can encounter before and after. Let them know how long the service typically lasts. And please, tell them the offering is just for members and regular attendees.

You should also explain your communion practices, since these vary a lot from one church to another. At most of the churches we visited that included communion, my desire to understand and fit in with their practices so distracted me that I failed to focus on the reason why I was taking communion. This was an epic fail for me—and for them.

Lastly, make it easy for prospective visitors to contact your church with questions. This includes listing your phone number and email address. Just make sure you respond quickly to both. Most churches don't, with a few delaying their response to visitor communication for days, weeks, and, in one case, even months. And some don't respond at all.

What I've *not* included on this list of website information is a doctrinal statement. I don't think most people care, and those who read it may seek one hot-button word or phrase, using it to eliminate your church from further consideration. The reality is that at most churches, the people who go there don't know what their church's core beliefs are, and those who do know, often disagree with an element or two.

Create a Great Impression

Okay, so your website did a good enough job to entice someone to visit your church. Now you need to make a great impression when they arrive, knowing that their first perception of your church began with your website.

You've given them your street address, so their GPS will get them to your facility. If you only have one entrance to your parking lot, they'll know where to go, but if you have multiple entrances, be sure to have signs, banners, or flags directing them to the right one. Some large churches have parking lot attendants to direct traffic to open spaces, but even some forward-thinking mid-sized churches have greeters in their parking lot to welcome visitors and be available to answer questions.

You must have someone greet them at your building entrance to give them a smile, welcome them well, and open the door. This person should focus on people they don't recognize and not their friends. This greeter should look for signs of apprehension or confusion, doing whatever they can to ease a visitor's concerns or fears.

A positive welcome, however, extends inside the building too. Larger churches have visible and attractive information centers, staffed by approachable and outgoing people to assist visitors in any way possible. At smaller churches, or those lacking the space for a visitor center, station people inside to assist those who look lost or confused.

In all this, the goal is to make a great impression,

welcoming visitors well and helping them enjoy their experience.

Greet Well

As I mentioned in *52 Churches*, there are three opportunities to greet visitors: before the service, during the service, and after the service. Few churches do all three well. And too many fail at each one.

As already mentioned, the pre-service greeting occurs in the parking lot, at the front door, and inside your facility. But that's not enough. These people serve as official greeters because they're outgoing, engaging, and have a knack at helping people feel comfortable. However, this doesn't mean the other 99 percent of your church shouldn't also greet visitors.

The pre-church greeting extends into the sanctuary or worship space. This secondary form of greeting could be as simple as making eye contact, smiling, and waving or saying hello. Anyone should be able to do that. Beyond that, everyone should look for people standing by themselves with no one to talk to or who look lost. Talking with friends should always take second place to interacting with visitors. And remember, most visitors won't care if someone's approach may be a bit awkward. They'll just be thrilled that someone cared enough to try.

For stoic churches, a nod of acknowledgment may be all you can do, while for more outgoing churches, the time before the service is a great opportunity to get to know someone. You can even offer to sit with them during the service to help them feel more comfortable and better navigate the service. This is extremely important for churches with liturgical services, which are hard for most visitors to follow.

Next is the greeting during the service. From a visitor perspective, most churches do this so poorly they might be better off skipping it. Seriously.

If you do have a greeting time during the service, train your people to be visitor-focused, not friend-focused. Give visitors the bulk of your attention. Make eye contact, smile, and offer a handshake. Share your name. Ask theirs. Now introduce them to someone else. And whatever you do, don't allow visitors to squirm in silence while everyone else is talking with others.

Don't call out visitors by having them raise their hand, or worse, stand up. This is most embarrassing. Instead, invite them to go to the back of the sanctuary or visitor center after the service.

The final greeting occurs after the service ends. It's true that some visitors scoot out as quickly as possible—especially if they had a bad experience—but other visitors may be open to tarry. Reward them for their bravery by talking to them. At the same time, don't overwhelm or interrogate them, just be friendly. Seek to establish a connection. If there's any after-church activity, invite them to stay for it. This may be coffee and refreshments. Or it could be a potluck. Assure them there will be plenty of food and that they're welcome to stay. Ask them if they have any questions. If you don't know the answer, take them to someone else who will be able to help.

Though not as common as it once was, you can invite them to have lunch with you.

Even if your church failed at the pre-church greeting and the mid-service greeting, a good post-church greeting can still salvage the situation, serving as a final and positive impression for them to take home.

Good worship music and engaging preaching may draw visitors, but it's the human connection that keeps them coming back. This starts with greeting visitors well.

Summary

If you want your church to grow—and every church should—strive to engage with visitors. This starts with the information you provide online, which should make it easy for them to decide to visit. It continues by making multiple good impressions when they arrive at your facility. Then it culminates with greeting them well before, during, and after the service.

You won't succeed in each of these areas every time, but you should work to succeed in as many of them as possible, as often as possible.

Takeaway for Everyone: Turn your focus from yourself and your friends to visitors and those you don't know.

HOW TO GO TO CHURCH

When going to church—whether as a visitor or a regular attendee—there are three keys to having a successful, meaningful, and spirit-filled experience. These are attitude, prayer, and expectation.

Without addressing these critical elements, many church services will fall short of expectations. Following these three essential steps, however, can make most any church experience—despite its shortcomings—positive, even beneficial, and, dare I say, memorable.

Yes, it is true. In visiting all these churches, I've experienced both positive and negative outcomes. And most of these outcomes hinged on attitude, prayer, and expectation.

Attitude is Everything

If we go to church with a bad attitude, we shouldn't expect to enjoy our time there. It's foolish to assume a positive outcome from church if we go there with a surly disposition.

When we approach church with positive anticipation of what will occur, our attention will focus on the positive elements of the service and give us the ability to extend grace to the negative aspects. Our attention will celebrate the noteworthy and give us the ability to overlook the not-so-great.

And remember, every church, congregation, and service will possess both positive and negative elements. No church is perfect in every way, just as no church is completely flawed. Our attitude determines which of those two aspects we focus on.

I approached most all the churches we visited with a positive perspective. Most of the time this came naturally. A few times, however, I needed to work on adjusting my attitude. Seeking a positive attitude means my overall approach to the church was positive. Even so, that doesn't mean I noted only positive elements. In visiting churches, I sought to share both positive and negative, celebrating the good that I witnessed and attempting to learn from the not-so-good that I encountered.

This is the reason I opted not to visit Church #69 ("Suffering from a Bad Rap"). From what people told me about their experience with this church and how the people who went there treated them, I formed a highly negative impression. Based completely on this secondhand information, I developed a bad attitude about this church and suspected my experience would confirm what I anticipated.

Since I had such a bad perspective, I saw no point in visiting them until I could turn my mindset from negative to positive. I tried unsuccessfully for a couple of years to adjust my attitude, but I never could. Therefore, I felt a visit would unfold as a futile encounter and produce no valuable insight or significant spiritual interaction.

I now realize—albeit too late—that I never prayed about this. I never sought the Holy Spirit's intervention to correct my flagging attitude. Through prayer, I'm quite confident God would have turned my attitude around. Unfortunately, I didn't think to seek him in this.

This brings us to the next point: prayer.

Prayer Is Essential

When Candy and I embarked on our *52 Churches* adventure, we committed ourselves to a pre-church prayer each week. Initially this was before we left our house, but later it occurred during our drive to church. Our intent was to seek God's blessing for our time with that church and to request a positive outcome. We only forgot to do this a couple of times, with our lack of prayer serving to diminish what we encountered at those churches.

So significant were the benefits of our pre-church prayer that we continued this practice when we weren't visiting a new church but instead were attending our home church. Most of the time I would pray, and Candy would add her addendum as she felt led. Other times I asked her to pray.

After a few weeks, I realized our pre-church prayer could easily slip into a rut, with us repeating the same phrases week after week. To avoid falling into a vain repetition (see Matthew 6:7 in the KJV), I would seek Holy Spirit insight on what specific things to pray for during our drive to church each Sunday.

As a way of example, and not to imply something for

you to copy, here are parts of some of our pre-church prayers:

- "Thank you, God, for the opportunity to go to church today. Please teach us what you would have us learn."
- "Papa, at church today may we receive what you want us to receive and give to others what you want us to give."
- "May we worship you today in spirit and truth" (see John 4:23–24).
- "Holy Spirit, direct us to divine encounters with the people at this church so that we may encourage them, and they may encourage us, as needed."
- "Please give us positive attitudes so that we may see what you want us to see." (I prayed this prayer a few times, but Candy clarified that she already had a good attitude. It was mine that needed adjustment. She was right.)
- "We thank you, Jesus, for who you are and what you've done for us. May we celebrate you today at church."
- "God, please speak to us through the sermon today."

As we returned to our home church, these types of prayers continued, though some new ones were a bit more pointed, as in:

- "Please direct us, Holy Spirit, to someone to minister to today at church."

- "May you give us opportunities to pray for others before and after the church service."
- "Father, today at church, may we see others through your eyes and encourage them in Jesus's name."

Use these examples to form your own pre-church prayers. But regardless of the words you say, know that prayer is essential when you head off to church. These prayers don't need to be fancy, but they should be heartfelt and Holy Spirit driven.

Prayer establishes the groundwork for what happens next.

Expectations Form Experience

The foundation formed by prayer prepares us for the church service. It serves to shape our expectations, which will drive our experience. Most of the time, positive expectations result in positive outcomes, while negative expectations prompt negative results.

With prayer establishing the basis to move forward, we should easily slide into a mindset of positive expectation. This is how we put our faith into action. We say our pre-church prayer in faith, and we prove it from the actions that spring forth from our expectations.

When we expect great things to happen at church, we will see the positive most every time. If we expect disappointment, we will surely encounter it.

As I said before, we will never experience a 100 percent perfect service, nor will we ever experience a 100 percent horrible one. Church experiences exist on a continuum from good to bad, positive to negative. And yet, when we walk in with positive expectations, our experience will skew toward the positive.

For most Sundays, our pre-church prayer did exactly that. Yet, on a few occasions, I needed to breathe a *booster* prayer as we pulled into the church parking lot, walked through the doors, or encountered some initial disappointment. These prayers sometimes came forth as little more than a groan, but God granted my plea every time.

Summary

Whether visiting a new church or attending our home church, we should follow a wise strategy, remembering that attitude is everything, prayer is essential, and expectations form experience.

May we receive God's blessing when we go to church, and while we're there, may we be a blessing to others.

May it be so.

Takeaway for Members: Go to church with the right attitude, covered with prayer, and with high expectations.

If you liked *More Than 52 Churches,* please leave a review online. Your review will help others discover this book and encourage them to read it too. Thank you.

WHAT BOOK DO YOU WANT TO READ NEXT?

Other books in the Visiting Churches Series:

52 Churches
Visiting Online Church
Shopping for Church
The 52 Churches Workbook
The More Than 52 Churches Workbook

FOR SMALL GROUPS, SUNDAY SCHOOL, AND CLASSES

More Than 52 Churches makes an ideal discussion guide for small groups, Sunday School, and classes. In preparation for the conversation, read one chapter of this book before you meet.

When you get together, pray and ask for Holy Spirit insight.

Discuss the key points of the chapter and explore the takeaway item.

- Celebrate areas your church does well.
- Consider a weakness that needs improvement.
- Determine what you can do to bring about positive change.

End by asking God to help you apply what you've learned.

For Small Groups, Sunday School, and Classes

May God bless you as you discuss this book and explore how to apply it to your practices.

ABOUT PETER DEHAAN

Peter DeHaan, PhD, wants to change the world one word at a time. His books and blog posts discuss God, the Bible, and church, geared toward spiritual seekers and church dropouts. Many people feel church has let them down, and Peter seeks to encourage them as they search for a place to belong.

But he's not afraid to ask tough questions or make religious people squirm. He's not trying to be provocative. Instead, he seeks truth, even if it makes people uncomfortable. Peter urges Christians to push past the status quo and reexamine how they practice their faith in every part of their lives.

Peter earned his doctorate, awarded with high distinction, from Trinity College of the Bible and Theological Seminary. He lives with his wife in beautiful Southwest Michigan and wrangles crossword puzzles in his spare time.

A lifelong student of Scripture, Peter wrote the 1,000-page website ABibleADay.com to encourage people to explore the Bible, the greatest book ever written. His popular blog, at PeterDeHaan.com, addresses biblical Christianity to build a faith that matters.

Read his blog, receive his newsletter, and learn more at PeterDeHaan.com.

BOOKS BY PETER DEHAAN

Visiting Churches Series:

52 Churches

The 52 Churches Workbook

More Than 52 Churches

The More Than 52 Churches Workbook

Visiting Online Church

Shopping for Church

40-Day Bible Study Series:

Dear Theophilus (the Gospel of Luke)

Acts Bible Study

Isaiah Bible Study

Minor Prophets Bible Study

Job Bible Study

Living Water (John)

Love Is Patient (1 and 2 Corinthians)

Revelation Bible Study

1, 2, & 3 John Bible Study

Hebrews Bible Study

James and Jude Bible Study

Matthew Bible Study

1 & 2 Peter Bible Study

Mark Bible Study

Holiday Celebration Bible Study Series:

The Advent of Jesus

The Passion of Jesus (Lent)

The Victory of Jesus (Easter)

The Ministry of Jesus

Thanksgiving with Jesus

New Year with Jesus

Bible Character Sketches Series:

Women of the Bible

The Friends and Foes of Jesus

Old Testament Sinners and Saints

More Old Testament Sinners and Saints

Heroes and Heavies of the Apocrypha

200 Old Testament Sinners and Saints

Other Books:

Elephant God

Jesus's Broken Church

Martin Luther's 95 Theses

The Christian Church's LGBTQ Failure

Bridging the Sacred-Secular Divide

Beyond Psalm 150

How Big Is Your Tent?

For the latest list of all Peter's books, go to PeterDeHaan.com/books.

www.ingramcontent.com/pod-product-compliance
Lightning Source LLC
Chambersburg PA
CBHW072016110526
44592CB00012B/1336